"My friend Jeff Manion reveals the truth about what it looks like to live a life of lasting significance. Jeff has lived a life of faithfulness, and I'm so grateful he has shared this journey with us in the pages of *Dream Big, Think Small*. Jeff gives us a beautiful vision for the joy that comes from living with intention."

—**Shauna Niequist,** author of *Bread & Wine*
and *Present Over Perfect*

"Jeff drops the checkered flag and proves once again that the turtle wins."

—**Brad Formsma,** bestselling author of *I Like Giving*
and the founder of Ilikegiving.com—a movement that
inspires people to live generously through stories

"*Dream Big, Think Small* is a refreshing back-to-the-heart look at a fruitful life. I personally was challenged, then encouraged through Jeff's chewable lessons of how God hides miracles in the common places."

—**Dr. Wayne Cordeiro,** New Hope Oahu

"Jeff draws from a deep well of biblical wisdom and compelling illustrations in his latest book: *Dream Big, Think Small*. Most significantly to me, he is living what he is inviting us to experience. As I read, I was inspired to pursue an extraordinary life with Jesus one day at a time."

—**Todd Harper,** President at Generous Giving
and author of *Abundant: Experiencing
the Incredible Journey of Generosity*

"The ideas in this book are both completely countercultural and utterly refreshing. We live in an era of 'superhero' stories, but Jeff's book makes it clear: The real heroes are the humble, the consistent, and the everyday faithful. I love this book."

—**Brant Hansen,** radio host and author of *Unoffendable*

"In a world where success outpaces character and people become famous overnight, *Dream Big, Think Small* is a clarion call to the kingdom of consistency, an invitation to a life of faithfulness over the long haul. Read this, live this, and your life will become fruitful in every season."

—**Steve Carter,** Willow Creek Community Church
Teaching Pastor and author of *This Invitational Life*

"*Dream Big, Think Small* advocates for a new way of thinking, and I couldn't love Jeff's approach more. His idea that big dreams are anchored in small life-giving habits has changed the way I think about achieving goals. With a storyteller's flair and a knack for providing takeaways you can actually use, this book will surely inspire you to be faithful in the commonplace because that is where the magic happens."

—**Mandy Arioto,** President and CEO
of MOPS International

dream big,
think
... small

ALSO BY JEFF MANION

Satisfied

The Land Between

dream big,
think
small

living an extraordinary life one day at a time

jeff manion

ZONDERVAN®

ZONDERVAN

Dream Big, Think Small
Copyright © 2017 by Jeff Manion

Requests for information should be addressed to:
Zondervan, *3900 Sparks Drive SE, Grand Rapids, Michigan 49546*

ISBN 978-0-310-32857-5 (softcover)

ISBN 978-0-310-32874-2 (audio)

ISBN 978-0-310-32859-9 (ebook)

Published in association with the literary agency of Wolgemuth & Associates,
Inc.

Cover design: Curt Diepenhorst
Cover illustration: © Maartje van Caspel / iStock®
Interior illustration: Kait Lamphere

Firsting printing November 2016 / Printed in the United States of America

CONTENTS

WEEK FOUR: LIFE-GIVING RELATIONSHIPS

WEEK FIVE: STRESS FRACTURES

WEEK SIX: REVISITING SUCCESS

THE MYTH OF OVERNIGHT SUCCESS

MY RÉSUMÉ IS FAIRLY SHORT BECAUSE, REALLY, I'VE held only one job. My wife, Chris, and I were married when we were both twenty-one, and we began serving Ada Bible Church in Grand Rapids, Michigan, a few months after our wedding. Now in our mid-fifties, we continue to serve the same ministry in the same community.

If overnight success actually exists—and I'm fairly confident it doesn't—we've never experienced it. During our thirty-plus years in ministry we've witnessed a handful of sudden breakthroughs as Ada Bible Church has grown from a couple dozen people meeting in a house to a thriving congregation serving thousands of lives. But without exception, these "sudden" breakthroughs were bracketed by years of faithfully plugging away.

A while back Chris and I visited the Wright Brothers National Memorial at Kill Devil Hills, just outside Kitty Hawk, North Carolina. There, on December 17, 1903, the two brothers made history when Orville Wright flew their plane 120 feet, staying aloft for twelve seconds. Later that day, Wilber piloted the aircraft 852 feet. The Wright brothers are celebrated as being the first human beings to achieve controlled flight.

Sudden success.

But explore David McCullough's book *The Wright Brothers*, and you realize the agonizingly slow business of getting that plane off the ground—years of tinkering, designing, experimenting, failing, adjusting, and trying again. Their work was so tedious that the residents of Dayton, Ohio—where many of their experimental flights occurred—were largely blind to the fact that history was being made just outside of town. If you had journeyed to the countryside to observe the phenomenon, you might have witnessed nothing more than two men tinkering with various airplane parts for weeks on end. There was nothing much to see. Moments of airborne awe were rare.

Listen to the assessment of Orville and Wilber's own nephew, who years later reflected, "History was happening in those moments, there in their shop and in their home, but I didn't realize it at the time because it seemed so commonplace."[1]

There it is. The invention that has, perhaps more than any other, shaped the last hundred years of human history. And the term to describe the achievement? *Commonplace.* It is human nature to celebrate the astounding breakthrough rather than the repetitive, tedious work that leads to the breakthrough.

As I reflect back on our own journey, I vividly recall the series of challenges that marked our first seven years of ministry as a handful of us struggled to get the church airborne. Then "suddenly" we took off (more about this on Day 4). The lessons from those early years have been affirmed again and again. Persistent faithfulness over an extended period of time has no substitute. When disappointed by painfully slow progress—or what feels like no progress—we're tempted to grow discouraged and quit. I'm so grateful we didn't throw in the towel during our unspectacular years of dependably plodding along.

I once heard Pastor Craig Groeschel address a generation of young leaders. He observed, "You'll likely overestimate what you can do in the short run but underestimate what you can do in a lifetime of faithfulness."

So true.

Most of us are not attempting to unlock the mysteries of flight. We lead families, companies, churches, and schools. We serve as nurses, coaches, sales reps, parents, and youth pastors. It is common to grow weary, bored, or even disillusioned as we pour ourselves into the people around us. But when big dreams are finally realized, it is through the steady devotion of bringing ourselves again and again, day after day, year after year to the little stuff. Success in the large things requires deep, abiding commitment to the small things.

I reflect on the gracious marriage built on the routine habit of swiftly apologizing when a minor wound has been inflicted. Or the exceptional hotel where every interaction with an employee ends with, "Is there any other way I can serve you?" I marvel when a lower-middle-class family builds a solid financial life through saving a bit of money from every single paycheck—for years. And I am overwhelmed with gratitude when I discover that this same family lives with radical generosity, giving away money from every single paycheck.

These are small things, really—saying "I'm sorry," offering to serve, being disciplined in saving and giving. But over time these small things accumulate to produce great marriages, great companies, and great lives.

I've written these words to encourage you to remain diligent in the small things. I invite you on a six-week journey with me to challenge the myth of overnight success and celebrate the life of steady faithfulness.

Your work matters. Your life matters. I encourage you to build an extraordinary life a day at a time. I pray that our gracious Lord will deliver you from the quest for a quick fix and that you will taste the joy and freedom that come from a life of consistent faithfulness.

Big dreams must be anchored in small, life-giving habits.

This is why I challenge you to dream big, but to think small.

HOW TO READ THIS BOOK

DREAM BIG, THINK SMALL FOLLOWS A SIX-WEEK READ-
ing plan. While the book can be read from cover to cover, I invite
you to chew on only one chapter a day, five days a week, for six
weeks. In this way the format of the book mirrors the message
of the book, and you can chip away at this message one day at a
time, both with the book and with your life.

It is my hope that this book will not only serve you personally
but also provide a great resource for those "Will you mentor me?"
situations. You know, the relationships that result in weekly meetings at a restaurant, where you invest in someone else's growth and
development. This tool can serve you as you develop faithfulness
in others and as you grow together.

WEEK ONE:

A CASE FOR STEADY MOVEMENT

NEWS FLASH: The Turtle Wins

The tale of the tortoise and the hare stretches back to ancient Greece, appearing in Aesop's collection of fables. The course is set, the race begins, and the hare dashes out of sight, only to stop and recline for a nap. The tortoise quietly plods on, passing the sleeping hare and crossing the finish line first.

What is the moral of this story from millennia past?

Slow and steady wins the race.

The lesson in this age-old tale is not found in the "slow" part of the story as much as it is in the "steady" part. Anyone can mosey along at a snail's—or tortoise's—pace for a time. But steady progress in a positive, holy direction requires tenacity. Endurance is demanded for those committed to a faithful, life-giving direction over months and years.

So in Week One, let's explore the power of steady progress. And together, over the next five days, we'll celebrate the virtue of slow and steady movement.

DAY 1:

A NEW KIND OF HERO

HEROIC MOMENTS

Normality aboard the high-speed passenger train from Amsterdam to Paris was broken by the explosion of gunfire and sound of breaking glass. The Moroccan terrorist Sliman Hamzi was armed with an assault rifle, an automatic pistol, and enough ammunition to inflict untold loss of life on the crowded train. But as he paused to adjust his rifle, three vacationing Americans rushed him. Spencer Stone, Alek Skarlatos, and Anthony Sadler tackled the gunman, beat him unconscious, and tied him up. Their swift, courageous response averted a massacre.

News of the heroic action was broadcast around the world. Days after the incident, the president of France, François Hollande, honored the Americans with his country's prestigious Legion of Honour for saving countless lives. Back in the States, the trio was invited to the Oval Office, where President Obama personally thanked them, extolling their courage and teamwork.

The accolades were not limited to recognition by heads of

state. The Los Angeles Lakers honored the three during a game, presenting them with team jerseys as enthusiastic fans gave them a standing ovation.

The attention was well deserved. These men had risked their lives to save others.

THE QUIET VIRTUE

Such instances of extreme heroism are rare in our world, though, because opportunities to risk our lives are limited. A person who desired to emulate this exact form of courage would have to spend a lifetime riding trains, hoping to spot a would-be terrorist. Then, if he or she did spot one, tackle him and tie him up. Favorable conditions for this kind of greatness just don't come along every day, and perhaps never in a lifetime. Lifesaving heroics depend on life-threatening situations, and you can't preschedule those into your week.

This reality is what the seventeeth-century French priest François Fénelon was getting at when he observed, "Great acts of virtue are rare because they are seldom called for."[1]

Heroic intervention—"great acts of virtue" in Fénelon's phraseology—is seldom required of us. But when these exceptional opportunities do present themselves, they tend to carry the immediate rewards of excitement and recognition.

In contrast to these rare heroic moments, Fénelon praises the recital of small acts of obedience practiced over and over:

To do small things that are right continually, without being noticed, is much more important. . . . Faithfulness in the little things better proves your true love for God. It is the slow, plodding path rather than a passing fit of enthusiasm that matters.[2]

This "slow, plodding path" of faithfulness in small things is not likely to grab news headlines or result in the presentation of an NBA jersey or recognition at the White House. Faithfulness is a quiet virtue. It doesn't make a lot of noise. We applaud endurance at the finish line, but those middle miles of plugging away are fairly uneventful. Commitment isn't flashy, and long devotion often goes unnoticed.

But faithfulness counts! It counts in marriages and in families and in ministries. Commitment matters. It matters in schools and companies and communities. The "slow, plodding path" matters because true lasting impact requires steady, consistent movement in a singular direction over a considerable period of time.

HONORING FAITHFULNESS

Around us are a myriad of faithful people quietly living out great lives with little hype or attention. While not flashy, their journey of faithfulness is worth living and celebrating.

Faithfulness is seen in the dedicated father who endlessly reenacts the bedtime ritual of reading to his children, sometimes the same book for weeks and weeks. He's steadily and consistently present for his young ones, providing a sense of security as the day draws to a close—and perhaps instilling a love of reading in the process. This kind of seemingly redundant love leaves a lasting imprint.

Faithfulness is visible in the married couple who direct the youth group for a growing congregation. They understand it may take five years of consistent ministry before a solid high school program fully takes root. And so they dig in for the long haul, loving and leading month after month, free from the delusion that an enduring foundation can be built in just a few months.

Faithfulness is also evident in a committed believer's daily, early morning, before-work ritual of employing a journal and Bible, with a mug of tea resting on the end table beside her chair in the sunroom. These quiet moments of introspection shape her heart and her life. She reads a chapter of the Bible, jots down observations in her journal, and invites God into her day. She's come to understand that a strong public life is built upon the foundation of a strong private life; so day after day, year after year, she listens to God in the early-morning stillness. Holiness is formed in this space. These quiet moments matter. They are unspectacular when observed from day to day, but over time they direct and shape our lives.

I agree with François Fénelon that it is faithfulness in the small things that best expresses our love for God. This is a different kind of greatness. This is a journey not marked by spectacular feats of stunning heroism but by a tenacious commitment to repeated goodness.

To the congregation he founded in southern Greece, the apostle Paul wrote, "Now it is required that those who have been given a trust must prove faithful" (1 Cor. 4:2).

Not brilliant, gifted, or popular. *Faithful.*

Greatness is accessible. You don't have to be an all-American athlete, a Rhodes Scholar, or a business mogul to live a truly great life. The journey is available to everyone.

I invite you to dream big, but to think small—to pursue a remarkable life by taking a thousand unremarkable steps. This doesn't mean the road will always be easy. The slow, plodding path requires perseverance, clarity, and an enormous amount of grace. The trip takes a new kind of hero, but it's a trip worth taking.

REFLECTION

As you complete Day 1, think of three people in your life who are examples of steady, consistent faithfulness. Write their names below and what you have learned from each of them. How can you apply what they've taught you to your own journey to dream big, but think small?

* _____

* _____

* _____

DAY 2:

ANT POWER

LET'S TALK ABOUT WHAT TO DO WHEN YOUR SIXTH grader asks for a drum set, why a marriage conference won't fix your marriage, and the reason reading the Bible tomorrow probably won't change your life. Sound like a lot to chew on? We'll get to it all . . . eventually.

But first, let's visit the ants.

Imagine a wise father guiding his eight-year-old son to an anthill. The father points to it and says, "Watch this with me." They kneel and observe the insects parading in and out of the earth. Back and forth they go, bearing tiny seeds.

The dad is desperate to make a lasting impression on his son. In the agrarian culture of Old Testament Israel, crops must be planted and harvested on time to avoid financial disaster. It's an unforgiving world where many families are only a drought away from poverty. The father knows what the son does not—that the family's survival depends on such ant-like discipline. This talk at the anthill is a life-and-death conversation.

As the boy watches the ants stream into the hill, his dad whispers, "Do you see that? They are tiny, and yet they know how to prepare for winter. In the summer, they gather seeds so they will have enough to eat when the weather grows cold." He pauses and solemnly adds, "We will be like the ants."

To fasten this lesson in the youngster's mind, he attaches a well-known proverb to the experience:

> *"Ants are creatures of little strength,*
> *yet they store up their food in the summer."*
> *(Prov. 30:25)*

ANT POWER

The wonder of the anthill rests in the contrast between the ant's size and its efficiency. Ants have "little strength," but they get the job done through consistent forward progress. King Solomon included this proverb on Ant Power to illustrate the accumulated effect of steady, repeated movement in the right direction. It's the power of consistency.

This isn't the only time these industrious insects make an appearance in Proverbs. In an early chapter of Solomon's collection, he addresses "the sluggard"—the lethargic character who seems incapable of resisting the gravitational pull of the couch. Immobilized by the tractor beam of laziness, the sluggard is unable to rouse himself. Life slips away as responsibilities go neglected and opportunities are lost.

Solomon's advice to this guy? Visit an anthill!

> *"Go to the ant, you sluggard; consider its ways and be wise!"*
> *(Prov. 6:6)*

Wisdom is gleaned by observing the steady, disciplined movement of the ant colony. Back and forth. Trip after trip. Consistent, redundant, methodical—and lifesaving. The ants remind us what can be achieved when we relentlessly chip away at the task before us.

Remember, faithfulness isn't flashy. The dynamic of Ant Power hinges on repetition. It might involve getting up and engaging in pretty much the same activity, over and over, week after week, year after year. But when measured over time, the effects of consistent, steady movement can be stunning.

DRUM SETS, MARRIAGE CONFERENCES, AND BIBLE READING

This brings us to the drum set.

My son Alex was in the sixth grade when he asked for a drum set. I almost said no because I imagined the drums collecting dust in a corner of our basement after his initial interest evaporated. But instead, in a flash of parental brilliance, I said if he came up with 50 percent of the money needed, his mother and I would eagerly foot the bill for the remainder.

I confess that I thought the odds were long that he would take me up on my offer and follow through. But the boy proved me wrong. He not only accepted my offer, but transformed into a miser, keeping a shoe box under his bed to stash a growing assortment of coins and bills. His hoard grew little by little, week by week. His allowance, birthday cash that arrived in the mail from benevolent grandparents, and money he earned by taking on additional tasks around the house all went into the shoe box. He grew this stockpile not suddenly, but bit by bit, dollar by dollar. His persistence shocked me.

It took him about a year to save his half, but he persevered and reached his goal. We were thrilled to follow through by covering the other half, and we also experienced immense joy as Alex developed into an exceptional drummer.

The consistent forward movement Alex embraced in saving the money for the drums is a great example of the steady pace of Ant Power. But the lesson from the anthill stretches far beyond a faithful savings plan. Ant Power can fortify any thriving relationship.

When a friend reflects, "That marriage conference saved our marriage," the reality is that it probably didn't. What usually happens when couples attend a marriage conference is that they open their hearts to a new insight or are convicted to begin a new behavior. Then, *following the conference*, they begin the slow and steady process of relating or responding differently. Over time—and it's often a lengthy period of time—they experience a stunning quality shift in their marriage. They determine to forgive more readily, listen more willingly, live more lovingly.

You know that saying, "The grass is greener on the other side of the fence"? My friend, the grass is greener where you take the time to water it.

I'm not implying that attending a marriage conference is a wasted weekend. Not at all. The conference can be huge, providing a catalyst for needed change. But powerful change rarely occurs over the course of a few days. The ant-like discipline following the conference is what proves essential to lasting transformation. Growth doesn't happen overnight.

This is why reading the Bible tomorrow morning probably won't change your life. Doing anything for just a day, even if it's positive, has an extremely limited effect. Dieting for a day, exercising for a day, saving part of one paycheck—you get the idea. It's not what we do once that marks our years with positive movement; it's what we do on repeat.

The Bible has 1,189 chapters. A person who quiets herself each and every morning, meditating on a single chapter of the Bible, will read through all the Scriptures in just over three years. If she devotes herself to this practice as a twenty-year-old, she will read through the Bible roughly ten times by the time she turns fifty. Some mornings will gloriously inspire thought-provoking movement. Others won't. In fact, on some days the reading will seem tedious and uninspiring. But the discipline of opening her heart each morning can grow wisdom that is attained only through long devotion. It's the slow and steady movement of Ant Power.

A WORD OF CAUTION

While Ant Power is required to build your life, it is not needed to destroy it. I know this doesn't sound fair, but although you can't build your life in a weekend, you *can* blow it up in a weekend.

A sexual indiscretion on a business trip severely cripples a marriage, leaving a spouse devastated and children reeling from the resulting earthquake. It can take years to build a reputation and only hours to dismantle one.

A second glass of wine gives way to a third. The flashing

lights, roadside Breathalyzer test, and resulting DUI can adversely affect your life for years.

A university student is expelled six months before graduation for plagiarizing in a paper.

What takes years of Ant Power to build can be destroyed in moments.

THE CHALLENGE

As we contemplate the slow and steady progress of Ant Power, here's a challenge for you. What is an activity or discipline you can devote yourself to day after day, week after week, year after year?

A friend of mine whose weight had become dangerously unhealthy decided to begin walking daily. At first his progress was unbelievably slow; walking even a couple of blocks was a challenge. After weeks of walking, however, he began to shed pounds and then began to jog in short segments. He is now an avid runner. His weight loss was not the result of a fad diet but the result of a new discipline he faithfully repeated over a lengthy period of time.

Don't expect to see massive change overnight. It's like the maple tree we planted in our front yard. There was little observable change from week to week, but a large, sturdy tree now sits where a stick was planted twenty years ago. Some of our most significant growth can be measured only after months or even years. So be patient. The small tasks you do over and over, week after week, again and again, do matter. The thousand unremarkable steps you take will be worth the journey.

REFLECTION

Consider one ant-like activity you could begin immediately. The list below is not exhaustive, but it might give you some ideas.

- Every day, sincerely thank someone at work for what they do.
- Walk or jog three days a week.
- Pray daily for your children or grandchildren.
- Begin a consistent savings program by setting aside money out of *every* paycheck.
- Faithfully give away a certain amount from every single paycheck.
- Read a chapter of the Bible each morning.
- Every evening, enjoy a book for at least thirty minutes instead of watching TV.

What ant-like activity can you begin today? Remember, it doesn't need to be spectacular or flashy. What's important is consistent, steady movement over a period of time. Choose an activity that will work for you, and write it down:

_____

_____

DAY 3:
MISTER ROGERS

CHRIS AND I WALKED DOWN HOLLYWOOD BOULEVARD, scanning the names on the sidewalk stars. Tom Cruise. Jack Nicholson. Johnny Cash. Meryl Streep. Leonardo DiCaprio, ABBA. Julia Roberts. Star after star, honoring the careers of film, TV, and music celebrities. And then I spotted the star I'd been searching for and posed for a picture beside it.

Fred Rogers. My hero.

Today the legacy of Fred Rogers lives on through the animated children's program *Daniel Tiger,* which I enjoy watching with my grandson Preston. But when I was a child, Fred Rogers appeared on the program *Mister Rogers' Neighborhood*, which aired daily on public television. If you are old enough to remember the program, you most likely recall how each episode began and can probably sing the opening tune.

A BEAUTIFUL DAY
IN THE NEIGHBORHOOD

Piano music begins, and Fred Rogers walks through the door with a smile and a wave, singing the theme song, "It's a Beautiful Day in the Neighborhood." His solo continues as he descends a short flight of stairs to the closet, where he exchanges his suit coat for a zip-up sweater. Then he sits on a bench, removes his dress shoes, and laces up his sneakers. With the wardrobe change complete, he finishes the opening number with the invitation, "Won't you be, won't you please, please won't you be my neighbor?"

This is how Fred McFeely Rogers opened his program for thirty-three years. Between 1968 and 2001, he embraced the redundancy of walking through the door and singing the same opening number while swapping out his dress coat and shoes for more casual attire.

So why the repetition? Why the same pattern day after day, week after week, year after year? I mean, wouldn't you grow bored, say, after maybe eight years of this? Now double that to sixteen years. Now double it again to thirty-two years and you're closing in on the length of time Fred Rogers repeated his opening sequence. Why would anyone choose such a tedious daily routine?

I suspect Fred Rogers reenacted his daily rhythm to model consistency. Many of his young viewers came from homes marked by structure and order. You know, homes where alarm clocks were set, breakfast was made, the dog was fed, and everyone dutifully went off to work or school. Later the grown-ups came home from work to make dinner, help with homework, and shuffle the kids off to bed. Daily order. Routine. Consistency.

Other viewers, however, knew little consistency or dependability. They came from homes marked instead by chaos and disruption, with no semblance of stability or predictable routine. I wonder if Fred Rogers served as the most dependable presence in many of these kids' lives by modeling his day-to-day consistency. Hang up your coat when you take it off. Tie your shoes when you put them on. We can employ certain rhythms and patterns and practices repetitively to make life work well. Fred Rogers modeled this through the daily rituals of his program.

Mister Rogers embodied dependability. He was faithfully present. He ministered, week in and week out, for an astounding thirty-three years. I do believe *minister* is the appropriate word to describe his impact. Fred Rogers was ordained by the Presbyterian Church to serve families through the medium of television. He donned the wardrobe of a servant each time he pulled on his sweater and laced up his shoes.

He believed the world was not a safe place and that children would discover this soon enough, experiencing the dark emotions of fear, loneliness, and grief. They needed a neighbor to help them process life. Fred Rogers devoted himself to being that neighbor—consistently, faithfully, dependably there.

THE LEGACY

The life work of my hero, Fred Rogers, did not go unnoticed.

His program attracted musical guests such as Yo-Yo Ma and Wynton Marsalis.

- *Mister Rogers' Neighborhood* was honored with four Daytime Emmy awards.
- In 1997 he received the Lifetime Achievement Award from the National Academy of Television Arts & Sciences.
- He was inducted into the Television Hall of Fame in 1999.

- In 2002, the year before his death, he was awarded with the highest civilian award an American can receive, The Presidential Medal of Freedom.

And for what? No slick computer imaging, no astounding graphics. We're talking sock puppets, my friends, with Rogers playing many of the parts himself. He also wrote and performed most of the music for the program, which was simple in melody and lyrics.

Why all the accolades and awards, then? I believe they were a result of his passionate commitment over an extended period of time. For years, he poured himself into the program with love, skill, and grace. Rogers harnessed the power of thinking small. His greatness rose from redundant faithfulness. He summoned creative energy for routine tasks. And he did it for decades.[1]

PASSIONATE LONGEVITY

I believe we can glean a major life lesson from the commitment of Fred Rogers. It deals with passionate longevity—not merely hanging around for a long time, but genuinely bringing our best selves to people for a sustained stretch of time. Life impact takes time.

It takes time to build trust.

It takes time to refine a skill set.

It takes time to build a solid reputation.

Don't miss the challenge embedded in the type of life influence I'm describing here. We generally don't leave our mark by lunging from one stunning achievement to the next. Much of our forward motion isn't all that interesting when viewed from day to day. It's only through weighing the collective sum of these repeated moments that such a life presses its profound imprint on the lives of others.

To what and to whom are *you* deeply committed? Far too many of us don't know. We dabble or flit from one interest to the next. From church to church, from job to job, and maybe from spouse to spouse. We quickly lose interest, or patience, and fly to the next new thing. Someday and somewhere, though, we'll need to land. We'll need to find our calling and then start doing the slow and steady work of building a legacy. Big dreams are only powerful when anchored in daily discipline. Dream big, think small. Be faithful in the ordinary again and again. And trust God to work in extraordinary ways if and when he chooses. Commit yourself to acts of daily service, and trust God with the results.

I'LL BE BACK

At the conclusion of each program Mister Rogers reversed the steps enacted in the introduction, putting on his street shoes and suit jacket and singing a closing number. His closing song changed over time, but in the later years of the program he sang,

> And I'll be back, when the day is new
> And I'll have more ideas for you
> And you'll have things you want to talk about.
> I will too.

Those four words—"And I'll be back"—typified his thirty-three-year run. He was back. Day after day. Week after week.

Month after month. Decade after decade. He was a dependable, faithful neighbor. I want very much to be like my hero, Mister Rogers.

REFLECTION

To what and to whom are you deeply committed? Find a pen and compose a short list. Your answer might include the names of family members—children, spouse, siblings, or parents. Or perhaps the church where you pour time, prayer, and financial support, or a nonprofit organization that has captured your heart and could capture your commitment. Vocational calling should anchor your list—how are you bringing passion and excellence to what often becomes "just a job"? Work consumes far too much of our lives to be merely survived or tolerated. Do you have a gift or ability that will flourish only by giving it time and energy?

To what are you devoted? To whom are you committed? Even if you're in a season of job transition or family upheaval, some commitments can sustain you and those around you. Take a moment to write down those commitments here:

_____

_____

_____

_____

DAY 4:

THE MOBILE HISTORY LESSON

IN HIS BOOK *HOW THE MIGHTY FALL,* BUSINESS ANALYST Jim Collins pronounces, "The signature of mediocrity is chronic inconsistency."[1]

The opposite of chronic inconsistency, of course, is chronic consistency—that character quality embedded in the word *faithfulness.* Yet many of us grow too easily bored taking the slow, plodding steps of a faithful life and are instead perpetually on the lookout for the Next Big Thing. We want to change the world—or at least our corner of it—but fail to effect significant change because we simply have not learned the power of consistently showing up. But remember, serving in a life-giving, transformational way often requires that we bring ourselves again and again—often in the same way, and usually to the same people.

Chris and I have served the community of Ada Bible Church for over thirty years. Today the ministry is a multi-campus church touching thousands of lives. But in the early years—for a *lot* of years—our people served diligently in an attempt to just keep the doors open. That era of struggle is important to our history and must not be forgotten.

This is why I frequently pile new staff members into a church van and take them on a tour of our former locations. I lead this "mobile history lesson" because, in a congregation our size, it's easy to become enamored by the Next Big Thing. I want those leading our ministries to embrace the discipline of thinking small—to comprehend that dreaming big is worthless if it's unaccompanied by a faithful, daily grind.

I long for our servants to cultivate tenacious dependability, to grasp the necessity of bringing themselves day after day—particularly in disappointing seasons when it seems as though nothing monumental is occurring. We take this historic drive not for me to wax nostalgic about our past, but to mark those qualities essential to our future.

Allow me to take you along on a typical mobile history lesson.

It's a beautiful June day as we climb into the fifteen-passenger van and pull away from our Cascade campus that serves around four thousand people each weekend. Today I am accompanied by eight of my coworkers who represent various ministries within the church—single adults, youth, music, missions, and small groups. These eight individuals have a couple of things in common. First, they are all new to our church staff, having entered their positions within the last year. Second, they are young, the majority in their mid-twenties, which means I've been doing this ministry thing longer than most of them have been alive.

Our drive will end at my home, where we'll enjoy lunch in the backyard, but I have intentionally selected a circuitous route to get there.

JOE AND NANCY'S HOUSE

We drive up a residential street and pause in front of a nondescript house. This, I explain, was the home of Joe and Nancy Smith, the couple who started Ada Bible Church four decades ago. The first services were held in their living room. The church struggled back then, moving from one temporary location to another and enduring the disappointment of seeing new, enthusiastic attendees grow weary and move on. The Smiths labored for seven years and resigned without achieving what they had hoped to accomplish. However, they did leave behind a solid core of about twenty faithful attendees.

This is where Ada Bible Church began.

THE YELLOW HOUSE

Our rolling history lesson continues as we drive a few more miles west. We pull off to the side of the road in front of another home. I explain that the unassuming yellow house across the street served as the meeting place for Ada Bible Church when I first preached there as a twenty-one-year-old college student. The building, now remodeled into a house, held seventy folding chairs. The basement served as our children's classroom.

The van idles as we stare at my past—our past. I recall how I preached in this building for five years, experiencing three deeply disappointing delays in a much-needed relocation. When we finally sold the building, the fifty or so attendees moved worship services to a nearby high school and then attempted to build a new facility with volunteer labor.

THE BLUE BOX

We drive to the corner, turn left, and proceed a mile to our next destination. This light-blue, two-story, boxy-looking structure was Ada Bible Church's home between 1990 and 1998. The auditorium seated perhaps two hundred people. On our opening weekend, we were overjoyed with the 115 people present for the inaugural service. I had now pastored the church for seven years, and my work followed the seven years of Joe and Nancy. That's fourteen years of dedicated labor to reach a consistent attendance of one hundred people.

I know a church that size is a remarkable achievement in some parts of the world. But not in Grand Rapids, Michigan, with a significant population center and an enormous number of people seeking a church experience. Our initial years were unspectacular by any measure, other than the singular virtue of perseverance. We didn't quit.

We exit the van and form a huddle in the parking lot as I share the challenges we weathered in this new era of ministry. After years of trying to get airborne, we experienced sudden growth. We moved to two services and then to three, surging past two hundred, five hundred, and then nine hundred attendees. In the process, we lost our identity as the small church family where everybody knew everybody else. This movement was jarring and awkward.

Imagine a thirteen-year-old who grows three inches over the summer—gangly and uncoordinated in last year's ill-fitting jeans. That was us.

In many respects, this transition didn't feel like a small church growing up as much as our small church dying to make way for a larger one. Growth comes painfully. Every time you gain something, you lose something.

Eight years into our wild ride in this blue, boxy building, we finally pulled the plug. We sold the facility and moved, once again, into an area high school as we engaged in a property search and started the challenging relocation process all over again.

LUNCH UNDER THE BIRCH TREE

We climb back into the van and drive to my home for lunch. It's a warm, early summer day, and Chris has prepared a delicious meal that we enjoy in the backyard. We sit at a rustic table beneath the shade of our birch tree, and we talk. Chris and I respond candidly to questions about disappointment, discouragement, and perseverance. We speak of our most fulfilling moments in ministry and talk openly about when we most felt like quitting.

This is not merely a history lesson. This conversation is about faithfulness. It's a dialogue about endurance—about the challenge of showing up again and again and again. My eight coworkers have joined the staff of a large church with a solid reputation. I want desperately for them to connect with the sweat and tears that were poured into Ada Bible Church when we were small, struggling to stay alive, and largely invisible to our community.

FAITHFUL STEPS

A legacy of faithfulness is what I desire for my coworkers—and the members of my congregation—and it's what I desire for you. If you aspire to be part of an outstanding business, church, school, camp, family—or even to build a life that has impact—there is no substitute for faithfulness over time. Yes, along your journey you may experience sudden breakthroughs. But these "sudden" surges are usually bracketed by lengthy periods of steady, faithful plodding.

Perseverance is hard. It's easy to grow impatient, restless, and bored. While faithfulness is not a sexy virtue, it *is* one of the most crucial. Explore the history of any healthy organization and you will discover, at its core, a nucleus of individuals who kept showing up.

People who end up changing their world—in ways big and small—are people who live a life of chronic consistency. They consistently show up, time and time again, usually in the same way and to the same people.

Truly great lives are born from steady, persistent steps in a singular, holy direction.

REFLECTION

As we complete Day 4, reflect on current challenges you are experiencing in work, ministry, or family. Is it possible that God is calling you to a season of faithfulness in the middle of this deeply challenging time? Write a brief description of your circumstances and a brief prayer—just a line or two—asking God to give you a faithful spirit in this season.

_____

_____

_____

_____

DAY 5:

THE TWENTY-MILE MARCH

IN 1911 TWO TEAMS OF EXPLORERS BATTLED THE ELE-
ments of Antarctica in a race to become the first human beings
to reach the South Pole. Great Britain's Robert Falcon Scott and
Norway's Roald Amundsen led their respective teams, each seeking
the honor of planting their country's flag at ninety degrees south.

The three-month trek in arctic conditions proved to be an
unbelievable challenge both physically and psychologically. The
teams battled bitterly cold wind, frostbite, meager rations, and
exhaustion as they crossed a seemingly endless expanse of white.
They not only competed with each other but were at war with
the brutal, unforgiving elements. Making it back alive would be
a remarkable achievement.

In *Great by Choice,* Jim Collins contrasted the strategies of
the two teams. Scott's team often chose to hammer out as many
miles as possible when conditions were favorable but hunker
down in their tents when the weather became brutal. Conversely,

Amundsen set a goal of trudging no more than twenty miles a day whatever the weather conditions were—exceptional, average, or horrible.

Their journal entries reveal the two mind-sets. During a particularly horrendous blizzard, Scott wrote, "I doubt if any party could travel in such weather." But when Amundsen faced similar conditions, he reflected, "It has been an unpleasant day—storm, drift, and frostbite, but we have advanced 13 miles closer to our goal."[1]

By covering as many miles as possible on the days the weather was more cooperative, Scott often drove his team to exhaustion. Amundsen, however, used the twenty-mile figure not only as a goal but also as a restraint. He would halt his team at midday when the maximum goal of twenty miles had been achieved, even if weather conditions were favorable and his team desired to push farther. He knew redlining physically could be lethal if they were caught in a blizzard or missed a supply depot in such a state of extreme fatigue.

Not only did Amundsen reach the South Pole first, he also returned safely to base camp with his entire team on the exact day he had predicted, traveling an unbelievable 1,860 miles in ninety-nine days.

Scott arrived at the South Pole to discover the Norwegian flag already planted there by Amundsen. Tragically, Scott and his exhausted team perished on their return trip, just eleven miles short of a lifesaving supply depot.

The steady, disciplined progress adopted by Amundsen serves as a compelling illustration of the power of moving consistently toward a meaningful goal.

Consider your own journey. To what consistent practices do

you give yourself day after day, whether sunshine or blizzard? What disciplines do you embrace whether or not you feel like it? What is your own twenty-mile march?

IT ADDS UP

The question is not about random activity but persistent movement. Our impact and influence are largely the result of our habits. It's not what we do one day; it's what we choose to do on repeat from one day to the next.

The irony is that, when viewed in isolation, no single activity looks particularly impressive. Reading to your child one evening. Volunteering for a weekend at your church. Putting a bit of money in savings before your paycheck evaporates. Taking a morning walk. Beginning a day with prayer. But allow these activities to become a pattern, a disciplined routine—a twenty-mile march— and over time the benefits amass. A legacy of faithfulness is born from small, repeated acts.

GIVING AWAY $100,000

One of the components of my twenty-mile march is consistent, faithful giving. It is a practice Chris and I committed ourselves to early in our marriage, and I am a bit stunned by its effect over time.

I once gave a high school graduation address about the impact of faithful movement in a holy direction. I offered insight on how to give away $100,000.

Our journey started with writing $40 checks. As newlyweds, Chris and I devoted ourselves to a practice called tithing—the discipline of restricting our spending to 90 percent of our income so 10 percent could be given away. We didn't decide to do this because we had money to spare. In our early twenties, as we worked to get our small church off the ground, our salary was tiny. This was also a time when our three children arrived in quick succession, and we struggled every month to buy basic groceries, put gas in the car, and make our small mortgage payment.

Writing these $40 offering checks stretched us considerably, but we persisted week after week, month after month, year after year. With a small church, growing children, and not a lot of financial margin, we still managed to give around $2,000 a year, or $10,000 over a five-year period.

Then, after years of struggling to get airborne, the church took off. Our salary increased as the congregation grew. As we moved into our thirties and forties, the size of our giving checks increased. I haven't done the exact math, but sometime in our early forties we crossed the threshold of giving away our first $100,000. What is remarkable to me is that the amount of our individual checks, taken alone, would not appear impressive. It is not the size of a single gift but the redundancy—the consistency—over a long period of time that builds a legacy of generosity.

Now, I don't intend for this practice to sound easy. It wasn't. But I'm so thankful we embraced the practice early. This was part of our twenty-mile march. We latched onto something good and committed ourselves to it.

So here's my advice on giving away your first $100,000. Get started immediately. Don't wait until you feel rich. Select a percentage of your income that stretches you and embrace consistent, systematic giving. Our journey started with writing $40 checks that stretched our faith. Where will yours begin?

ONE DAY AT A TIME

What we experienced with our twenty-mile march in financial giving holds true with exercise, serving, Bible reading, and parenting.

What legacy will you build one day at a time as you embark upon your own twenty-mile march? What seems too big for you to tackle all at once? Legacies aren't built in a day. They grow over time, step by step, mile by mile, and day by day. Dream big, think small. Success in the large things requires dependable commitment to the small things.

REFLECTION

As we close out Week One, it is important to put these ideas about persistent faithfulness into practice. Right now, think of that seemingly too-big-to-conquer goal and plan the first step of your twenty-mile march. Focus on steady progress. To what holy discipline will you give yourself consistently, whether sunshine or blizzard?

_____

_____

_____

WEEK TWO:

REFILLING AN EMPTY TANK

RUNNING ON EMPTY

I just filled the tank on my Subaru. Driving around the last couple of days, I've watched the needle on my gas gauge drop steadily toward E.

If you've been driving for any length of time, you know this is fairly automatic. A nonevent. You glance at the gauge, calculate how far you can drive, and think of when and where to fill up before your car abruptly sputters to a stop.

Gauging our spiritual and emotional reserves is far more complex. We have a tendency to "run on empty" without realizing it. When running on fumes, our mood sours, our creativity evaporates, and we find it challenging to make basic decisions.

If we want to love and serve faithfully over a lengthy period of time, we must become specialists at refreshing our weary spirits. So this week let's focus on filling the tank.

DAY 6:

QUITTING BEFORE THE FINISH LINE

A FEW SUMMERS AGO I SAT LISTENING TO HUEY LEWIS at an outdoor concert. Back in 1985, one of his hit songs, "The Power of Love," anchored the soundtrack to the movie *Back to the Future*.

Before performing the number that evening, Lewis said, joking, "When I wrote this years ago, I had no idea I would have to sing this song every day for the rest of my stinking life." The crowd laughed. Then the punch of the opening notes blasted from the stage and Lewis brought it! Even though he had performed the number hundreds of times before, he refused to phone it in. He belted out the song with energy, and we felt that we had been given a gift.

I love encountering people who bring energy and passion to their work long after initial enthusiasm has burned off.

Where have you seen this? It's visible in the teacher pouring creativity into her lessons when well past her twentieth year as an educator. I've witnessed it in my family doctor who thoughtfully engages patients when he walks through the door of an examination room, although he's done it literally thousands of times. You detect it in the gray-haired carpenter who still cares whether the house he's framing is square.

To be excited about one's work when it is new and fresh is one thing. To bring ourselves to tasks we've been doing for years is something else entirely.

I have long known that thirty years in a vocation do not automatically translate into three decades of passion. Just because we do something for a long time doesn't mean we excel at it. In fact, as the years compound, we can grow bored, disillusioned, or cynical. The amount of time on the line can work against us, slowly jading us. Numbing us.

WHEN DID YOU QUIT?

In businesses, schools, churches, and families, we tend to quit long before we reach the finish line. Discouraged and disillusioned, we zone out, numb out, or check out.

Is it possible that you are still married, but you gave up on your marriage years ago? Are you in the same house, but you emotionally abandoned your spouse long ago? Are the two of you going through the motions of being a married couple, trying to make everything look okay to the outside world while things are falling apart inside?

Did you stop parenting years before your child moved out of your home? Did the challenges of adolescence cause you to throw in the towel? Do you remember an altercation or deception or insult when you silently—or perhaps not so silently—vowed "I'm done!"?

Do you recall a deeply disappointing conversation when your boss, board, or ministry squashed The Best Idea Ever? What happened in your spirit that night and in the ensuing weeks? Is it possible that your body still occupies the office several days each week, but you stopped giving your heart months or years ago?

Somewhere along the line, did you quit before you reached the finish line?

FINISHING STRONG

Now in my mid-fifties, I increasingly ask legacy questions that weren't on my mind when I was twenty-five. Namely, what kind of old guy do I desire to become? If I am granted health and presence of mind, what kind of energy, heart, and creativity will I offer at, say, age seventy?

The term "finishing strong" has become overused to the point that it seems cliché. But as a runner, and as a pastor moving into his fourth decade in ministry, the term conjures a powerful image for me—a picture of not bailing when the race gets tough but of crossing the finish line.

I don't want to simply endure ministry, marriage, and friendships. I want to remain fully engaged—bringing the best version of myself to the needs of those around me. I don't want to ever become a guy standing behind a lectern uttering mechanical, formulaic, pathetic words that lack comfort, power, and challenge. I don't want to quit before I finish.

I don't believe passion can be maintained indefinitely. I think it needs to be restored. I reflect on the encouragement the apostle Paul wrote to the younger pastor Timothy, using the metaphor of fire: "I remind you to fan into flame the gift of God. . . . For the Spirit God gave us does not make us timid, but gives us power, love and self-discipline" (2 Tim. 1:6–7).

Paul's image of fanning dying embers into a flaming fire is powerful. Sometimes the fire begins to die out, and we need fresh movement of air for the flames to burn brightly once again. What events, friendships, and practices rekindle your fire and restore your passion for life? The goal is not only longevity, but passionate faithfulness over time. Not just showing up, but bringing the best version of ourselves to others.

In Week One we explored the quality of steady faithfulness. Now, in Week Two, we turn our attention to the challenge of restoring vitality over an extended period of time. In the next chapters we'll talk about how to refill an empty tank. If you pour yourself into others day after day, week after week, year after year, you will become drained. What will you do to restore your energy and passion? The answer to this question will determine the joy you bring to others five, ten, or twenty years from now. You don't have to reach a point where you're phoning it in. You can finish strong.

REFLECTION

Before closing out Day 6, please read this prayer aloud:

Gracious God, I need your refilling so badly in my life. Life drains me. People drain me. To serve faithfully with love and passion, I need you to restore my soul.

Please refill my life so that out of the resources you provide I can graciously fill others. I don't want to live a passionless life.

I ask for your wisdom with my thankfulness for all you provide.

DAY 7:

AID STATIONS

I SETTLED IN AT A COFFEE SHOP TO READ AND JOURNAL. It was the perfect, peaceful setting to quiet my heart and reflect on life. But my tranquility was quickly disrupted by the onset of a throbbing headache. I've experienced this dull throb before, and as soon as it started I knew exactly what was happening and why.

Earlier in the morning I'd taken off on a long training run in the damp November air. The temperature was chilly and I overdressed. I warmed up during the run and overheated a bit. I wasn't particularly thirsty and didn't drink anything during the run, or when I reached my car, or when I got home. Big mistake.

Returning home, I showered, gathered my journal and laptop, and headed to the calm of the coffee shop. That's when the dehydration-induced headache began to rob me of focus. I approached the counter and requested a glass of water, then another. But dehydration takes time to remedy, and the headache grew. The pain didn't fully dissipate for hours.

I've made this mistake before and probably will again. The lesson is simple: Don't wait until you are thirsty to drink. Know what your system needs, and act accordingly. In a prolonged endeavor—a long hike, bike ride, or run—take in water before you grow thirsty. If you wait until you are parched, you've probably waited too long. Unfortunately, we usually discover what we should have done after we didn't do it.

My coffee-shop headache serves as a parable for emotional depletion and the need to replenish ourselves. Serving a family, a company, or a ministry depletes your emotional reserves. If you are constantly pouring yourself out, you require a regimen of filling yourself up—rehydrating, if you will. Every "mile" of serving takes something out of you. If you want to live and love faithfully for decades—marathon distance—you had better know how to consistently restore depleted resources. And preferably before you are in desperate need.

The lesson is clear. Don't wait until you feel a searing headache and then begin your search for water. Drink before you are thirsty. Let's talk about ways to fill your spirit long before you grow emotionally, spiritually, or relationally dehydrated.

TIME AWAY

Don't wait for the compounding symptoms of emotional burnout before you justify a vacation or build rest into your schedule. Plan time away long before you experience a crash. Once you're totally depleted and drained, a week away isn't enough to repair the frayed ends of your weary life.

During a complicated season in Jesus's ministry, as enthusiastic crowds clamored for his attention and resentful enemies badgered him, he chose to get away with his apostles. "Come with me by yourselves to a quiet place and get some rest" (Mark 6:31). Read his words again. Hear them as a personal invitation. We all have intense seasons when we need to get away to a quiet place and rest. And also, remember that some trips aren't restful. You're probably familiar with the type of getaway that causes you to need a vacation to rest up from your vacation. Years back we pulled the plug on a complicated road trip and instead rented a simple lake cottage not far from our home.

DAILY RETREATS

Don't wait for a vacation to recharge your batteries. Nourish yourself daily.

In Week Three we will explore a story where Jesus took a retreat in the middle of a frantic weekend of serving people. "Very early in the morning, while it was still dark, Jesus got up, left the house and went off to a solitary place, where he prayed" (Mark 1:35).

Embrace the practice of the daily retreat. Seek quiet moments to reflect on Scripture, express gratitude for the blessings that surround you, and invite God into your challenging relationships and decisions.

Don't wait until you find yourself in the middle of a spiritual desert to refill your tank. Create space to fill your thirsty spirit each and every day.

LIFE-GIVING FRIENDSHIPS

Make space for life-giving friendships. Who are your true friends, and how does your calendar reflect your devotion to them?

On occasion, Jesus taught thousands of people. But he also

had an inner circle he limited to twelve disciples, and among those, had an even closer relationship with Peter, James, and John. Jesus also often visited the home of siblings Mary, Martha, and Lazarus in Bethany. Because their village was only a couple of miles from Jerusalem, Jesus could find refuge among trusted friends while encountering hostility in the capital.

Life can be lonely, but we make it lonelier than it needs to be by expending our life energy among a hundred shallow acquaintances while neglecting to connect deeply with any one individual. Don't wait until you are relationally famished to invest in life-giving friendships.

HEALTHY FAMILY

All you have to do for family relationships to erode is nothing. Relationships slide downhill by gravitational force in the routine wear and tear of life. How are family members prioritized in your busy life? Schedule downtime together, an occasional weekend away, a weekly date night with your spouse, or breakfast with one of your children. Create time to sit and eat and laugh. Invest in each other long before stress fractures are visible. Seek help early, before someone is ready to call it quits. Hydrate before a massive headache lets you know that you didn't.

ENERGIZING ACTIVITIES

What energizes you? Walking, painting, sailing, time with grandkids? What activities recharge your batteries, and how do you give these activities priority in your schedule? It isn't selfish to invest in your emotional health. When I am running on fumes, slogging through life in a perpetually depleted state, I am not leading, serving, or loving at my best. Life is draining. We need to discover ways to fill ourselves long before we crash.

Road races of any length have aid stations along the way. Volunteers fill thousands of cups with water or Gatorade. These tables are placed at predictable intervals along the course, with race maps letting you know exactly where you will find the aid stations. I think this is a great image of how to prepare for keeping ourselves hydrated in all parts of our lives.

Remember these words of Jesus to his disciples: "Come with me by yourselves to a quiet place and get some rest" (Mark 6:31).

Know where the aid stations are. Drink before you are thirsty. Don't wait for a meltdown or a breakdown before you refill your tank.

REFLECTION

Before closing out today's reading, pull up your calendar.

Look ahead four weeks to discern where the aid stations can be scheduled into your life. Over the course of the next month, where can you spend unrushed time with family or close friends? Where can you capture quiet moments to sit, read, and reflect?

Schedule these now. Write them into your calendar before every moment is claimed by draining activity.

Now look ahead three months. Where can you carve out significant time away? Schedule these times of rest long before routine commitments and demands stake a claim on every breathing moment.

DAY 8:

THE ART OF REST

WE AWAKEN LATER THAN USUAL ON A FRIDAY MORNING in October. I offer to take Chris to breakfast , but she opts for breakfast at home. When I was twelve, my mother died, leaving behind a bereaved pastor with five children. Until my father remarried, I was assigned the daily chore of making breakfast for the family. Other than grilling steaks, this is my sole culinary skill, and I enjoy it immensely.

I mold potato pancakes from leftover mashed potatoes, browning them in our seasoned cast-iron skillet. In another pan, I sauté onions and then stir in eggs and sausage for a scrambled egg concoction.

It doesn't feel like work to me. It's something I get to do.

It is an unrushed beginning to a slow, unencumbered day. Friday is our Sabbath.

I preach on Saturday evening and twice on Sunday. Speaking three times and interacting with scores of people, I find these weekend services emotionally and psychologically draining. For me, the traditional "Lord's Day" is not exactly a day of rest.

So years ago we chose Friday as the day we devote to getting nothing done. It's our day of intentional rest. Other days may be measured by what we accomplish. But Friday is different. It is the one day a week we awaken and announce, "There's nothing we have to do, no place we have to go." It's a day of "get to" rather than "have to."

Following breakfast, we decide where to walk. Our usual choice is a stroll through historic neighborhoods in Grand Rapids, ending at a coffee shop to journal or read. But today we choose a hiking trail not far from our home. We drive to the trailhead and ascend a leaf-strewn path into the woods. Autumn in West Michigan is magnificent, and today's colors are brilliant. Chris notices things I miss and draws my attention to deep-red maple leaves.

We believe these Sabbath walks repair and restore something crucial in our lives. Our tanks run dry. Stepping away from draining meetings and emails to walk and enjoy the world around us refills our empty tanks.

FREEDOM FROM THE GRIND

Chris and I find our Friday ritual liberating. We can't imagine fulfilling our calling with sustained joy and energy without observing these days of rest. Our Sabbath is a break from the grind, preventing every day from feeling like every other day.

Stepping off the treadmill for twenty-four hours provides a weekly finish line. When we begin to drag from the weight of life and work, rather than looking ahead and thinking, "Well, we do have vacation coming in a couple of months," we know a break is coming every seven days. A day to unplug and disconnect. A

Friday Sabbath that offers life-giving rhythm and freedom from the daily routine.

OUT OF EGYPT

This rhythm finds its origin in the heart of our Creator. As the Israelites exited slavery in Egypt and prepared to enter the land of promise, they were instructed to abandon work one day a week. Their directions from God read:

> Six days you shall labor and do all your work, but the seventh day is a sabbath to the LORD your God. On it you shall not do any work, neither you, nor your son or daughter, nor your male or female servant, nor your ox, your donkey or any of your animals, nor any foreigner residing in your towns, so that your male and female servants may rest, as you do. (Deut. 5:13–14)

Everybody gets a break! Kids, servants, immigrants—even the livestock. Everyone gets to shut down once a week and loosen their grip on productivity. And what is the rationale for this disruption of achievement? "Remember that you were slaves in Egypt and that the LORD your God brought you out of there with a mighty hand and an outstretched arm" (Deut. 5:15).

For generations, the children of Israel were forced to work seven days a week, never getting a break from the demands of their slave masters. A wild irony? We are prone to do willingly what the Israelites were forced to do as slaves. We chain ourselves to our work.

So once a week I cut the chains. I take a breather from endless demands and organizational decision-making and attempt to simply enjoy God's goodness. For me, it's the one day a week when I am not trying to fix the world. Untethered from production, I find myself more capable of being present to friends and family.

PENCILS UP

Sabbath is not my reward for getting all my work done. It is a break in the middle of my work.

If I wait until all my tasks are complete, I will never rest, because they're never done. Think of a standardized test like the SAT, where you have a certain time limit for each section. When the time has expired, the facilitator says, "Pencils up." You may have six questions yet to complete, but you're done—even if you're not done. From time to time, I arrive at Thursday evening and literally whisper, "Pencils up." I have emails unanswered, a weekend sermon unfinished, and various projects in midstream, but I'm done! Or at least done for now. Pencils up.

I've picked up a few insights over the years about practicing Sabbath. I share these in the next chapter with the hope that you will find my musings helpful as you work to establish a Sabbath rhythm in your own life.

But for now, I challenge you to consider that you were made for more than achievement. You are not the sum of what you produce. You are more than the number of cars you sell or the loads of laundry you fold or the quota of widgets you manufacture.

Our gracious Lord blends work and rest, productivity and

non-productivity, in a life-giving balance and rhythm that finds its origin in the heart of our Creator.

REFLECTION

Work punctuated by rest. What could such a rhythm look like for you? As you begin to contemplate the idea of practicing Sabbath, write down a few simple steps you can take to step away from your busyness. How could Sabbath rest bring greater balance to your life?

_____

_____

_____

_____

_____

_____

_____

DAY 9:

A LIFE-GIVING RHYTHM

I DON'T CONSIDER MYSELF AN EXPERT ON SABBATH rest. As I described our leisurely October Sabbath in the previous chapter, with its slow pace, home-cooked breakfast, and hike in the autumn woods, I don't mean to give the impression that Sabbath rest has come easily to me. It took a long time—a year, perhaps—to discover what this day would look like for us.

Others have likened the process to the challenge of learning a new musical instrument. It often takes time and experimentation to learn a life-giving Sabbath rhythm. It doesn't happen all of a sudden. Small steps, taken faithfully each week, add up to a satisfying and restoring pattern of weekly rejuvenation.

CHANGING SPEEDS

I think much of my learning curve had to do with the challenge of changing speeds.

When you're flying down the freeway exceeding seventy-five

miles per hour and then you follow the exit ramp into a small town with a twenty-five-miles-per-hour stretch through Main Street, it feels like you're crawling. "I could walk faster than this!" you think. In the same way, practicing Sabbath will feel strange for a while. When we race through life, changing speeds takes some getting used to.

But don't give up if it feels awkward and clumsy at first. It might take half a year of practice to begin to enter a rhythm that feels right. Practice, fail, improve, learn, and grow. Keep at it, knowing that the rhythm of work punctuated by rest was designed by your Creator for your benefit.

In describing what's worked for me, I'm not prescribing what it should look like for you. I'm merely sharing some ideas from my own experience. I urge you to explore and experiment and see what works best for you.

STOPPAGE

The concept of Sabbath is a stoppage of labor. We cease doing what we've been so busy with the other six days. Within that broad description, you may discover dozens of ways to slow your pace and enjoy God's goodness. Listening to music, taking walks, enjoying dinner with friends, participating in public worship, reading, writing, reflecting, playing board games, or working a puzzle just scratch the surface. As you explore Sabbath rest and try out various activities and non-activities, I trust you will discover certain practices that bring rest to your soul and rejuvenation to your spirit.

Because Sabbath is a stoppage of labor, much of my Sabbath practice can be described by what I cease doing. Chris and I have agreed to avoid certain activities on our Sabbath days. Because they derail our rest, we take them off the table for the day. Again, these aren't Sabbath rules that you should also observe but only a description of what we have found helpful.

WE AVOID OTHER WORK

On our Sabbath Fridays, we resist the temptation to replace our vocational work with other forms of work. For us, Sabbath is a day with no "to-do list." Often, people who observe a "day off" tend to merely swap "to-do lists." They detach themselves from one type of labor to attach themselves to another. Grocery shopping, car maintenance, and bill paying. Mow the lawn, get a haircut, select carpet and paint colors for the home renovation—the list never ends.

Ideally, we don't awaken on Friday morning with a list of things we have to get done. The ideal day would usher in the thought, "Today there's no place we have to go. Nothing we have to do."

But when do we race around to get everything accomplished? We have six other days to do that, and we attempt to get stuff done on those other days. The Sabbath, though, needs to be unlike those other days. It is a day without a list.

WE AVOID RACING AROUND

As we grew to love our unencumbered Sabbath Fridays, we began to anticipate what needed to be completed by Thursday evening. If we were to enjoy our Sabbath without racing around, we had to prepare. I didn't want to begin our day of rest searching for my bike pump so I could inflate my tires before a leisurely ride, then run by the gas station because my car's gas tank was almost empty, then hit an ATM down the street to secure needed cash. Suddenly a day of rest begins with an obstacle course of activity. And most of that activity could have been anticipated and done ahead of time.

Attempting the discipline of Sabbath often requires planning ahead a bit. So ask yourself the question, "What do I need to do today if I am to rest tomorrow?" And then figure out what you can do in advance so your Sabbath experience is more fully enjoyed.

Preparation might include setting out the kids' church clothes on Saturday evening so your Sunday morning departure doesn't include a scavenger hunt for lost shoes. Or scanning the fridge for the basics so the "leisurely morning" of the next day does not begin with a grocery run. Perhaps you load your backpack with hiking gear and prepare snacks ahead of time so you can set out on your adventure right away.

It took me a few months, but little by little I got better at planning ahead. I don't want my Sabbath day to begin with "have to's" before I can enjoy the "get to's," so I plan.

WE AVOID SHOPPING

Generally, we avoid shopping on our Sabbath Friday. I'm not talking about buying coffee and a scone or wandering through an antique store. I'm talking about intentional, planned acquisition—like shopping for a new coat, a new grill, or new furniture.

Here's my rationale for this. I tend to find my identity in my work. On Sabbath, through setting my work aside, I'm reminded that I am not the sum of my accomplishments. I enjoy God's goodness without trying to validate my existence through achievement.

But when I set aside my identity as "achiever," I may swiftly look for another flawed form of identity—namely, "consumer." If my identity is not found through what I achieve, perhaps it is attained in what I accumulate. For me, it's the temptation to replace one idol with another. That's why I've chosen not to intentionally shop on my Sabbath.

So on Sabbath Fridays we endeavor to enjoy what we already have—books and clothes and gadgets already in our possession. It is a day intended for relaxing in God's goodness, not succumbing to the illusion that another purchase will fill the empty space in us.

WE AVOID FINANCIAL CONVERSATIONS

We also attempt to stay clear of BIG FINANCIAL CONVERSATIONS—you know, the kind that can lead to arguments. Throwing a budgeting discussion into the middle of a peaceful car ride or summer walk is almost guaranteed to ambush serenity. We have six other days to talk about saving, selling, buying, and investing. On our Friday Sabbaths, we try to give it a break.

WE AVOID VACATION FANTASIES

Another type of activity I strive to avoid is shopping for vacation opportunities online. You know, scheming about some future getaway or reading travel reviews about a distant resort.

When I'm slogging through the daily grind or just plain worn-out, I can fantasize about getting away. Do you see the sad irony here? It's Friday! A full day dedicated to refreshing my spirit and, instead, I stare at a computer screen dreaming about refreshing my spirit. I remind myself, "I have *this* day to enjoy! Don't dream about getting away, Jeff. Just get outside—walk, explore. Don't think longingly about getting away from it all. You have *today*. You *are* away from it all!" Don't lose the here and now by dreaming about the there and then.

REALITY CHECK

As I've described taking a day off each week, you might be saying in protest, "There is no way I could pull that off every week! Life is way too complex."

In all honesty, Chris and I pull this off about half the time. We routinely have our Sabbath interrupted by weddings or wedding rehearsals, funeral home visitations, graduation open houses, or occasional speaking commitments that land on Fridays. On those days, we attempt to observe a half day, or even a few hours, of unobligated time.

We gave up the ideal of perfection long ago, realizing that the rest of our world doesn't come to a screeching halt because we decide to idle. We practice Sabbath imperfectly. We give ourselves grace. We strive for fully uninterrupted days and enjoy them immensely when they come our way.

On those days when our Sabbath is compromised by an obligation or event, we attempt to approach those responsibilities in a leisurely way, trying to maintain the spirit of our Sabbath day.

We often avoid the freeway, taking back roads to our destination or stopping along the way to discover a new café or coffee shop. In this way, we manage to observe a slower pace even when events encroach on a full day off.

I believe that by learning to find rest one day a week, I'm guided to find rest the other six days. Each and every day, my Lord whispers, "Come to me . . . you who are weary and burdened, and I will give you rest" (Matt. 11:28). Our Sabbath day reminds us that we are more than what we achieve or produce. And this reality needs to spill over into the other six days of the week.

From time to time, when someone learns I have served the same church for over thirty years and detects that I still approach ministry with passion and energy, they ask, "How do you do it?" The full answer is varied and complex, but I always seem to mention our Fridays. I think our practice of unplugging once a week is life-sustaining. I can't imagine going the distance without it.

Sabbath rest helps refill me. It empowers me to serve with greater joy and peace. It is care for my private world that encourages passionate longevity in my public world. When you slow your pace to enjoy God's goodness and drink in his creation, you discover a life-giving Sabbath rhythm—a rhythm of work punctuated by rest that helps you continue on the journey.

REFLECTION

As you consider how you will order your Sabbath and find balance in the rhythm of work and rest, jot down answers to the following five questions:

1. Do you have a designated Sabbath day?

_____

2. What activities (or non-activities) quiet your spirit and draw your heart toward rest?

_____

_____

_____

3. What barriers or obstacles prevent you from observing "down days"?

_____

_____

_____

4. What kind of advance preparation could make your Sabbath more restful?

_____

_____

_____

5. If you've never experimented with this life-giving practice, when can you begin?

_____

DAY 10:

RECOVERY

THE FIRST EMOTION I EXPERIENCE IS PROFOUND SADness flavored with light depression. It seems so wrong to feel this way. Here I am, alone at a friend's cottage, enjoying the beauty of the peaceful lake—a reprieve from the office, the appointments, and the decision-making. I've carved out three full days of solitude to rest my soul. To sleep late, read, and write. The setting is idyllic and my heart is unrushed for the first time in . . . how long? And then day two, as if on cue, sadness appears at the door, invading my tranquil retreat.

I've learned to anticipate the arrival of this uninvited guest. My theory is that when you are driving ninety miles per hour, you stay ahead of much of the pain. But pull into a rest stop, and disappointment catches up and parks beside you. Disappointment in others. Disappointment in yourself. Others' disappointment in you. People you cared about who moved out of your life. Sadness over unmet expectations. And weariness. Sometimes you don't realize how tired you've become until you stop moving.

These melancholy visitations announce the heart's cry for

recovery. After major events or an unbroken string of demanding challenges, the soul pleads for repair. It shouldn't surprise us that an emotional letdown awaits us after we pour ourselves into a demanding season.

THE MINISTER'S FAINTING FITS

Over a hundred years ago, the famed London pastor Charles Spurgeon touched on this theme when addressing students preparing for ministry. In his lecture "The Minister's Fainting Fits," he warned his students about the discouragement and depression that routinely visits those faithful servants who pour themselves out on behalf of others.

> Our work, when earnestly undertaken, lays us open to attacks in the direction of depression. . . . How often, on Lord's-day evenings, do we feel as if life were completely washed out of us! After pouring out our souls over our congregations, we feel like empty earthen pitchers which a child might break.[1]

I'm certain pastors reading Spurgeon's words can resonate with his description of Sunday evenings: washed out, emptied, and fragile. But the sensation of being completely drained is not unique to those of us with weekly preaching responsibilities. This bone-tired weariness is tasted by relief workers serving in the wake of a natural disaster or by trauma nurses administering crisis care. Fatigue is the common reality of camp staff nearing the end of an insanely busy summer, along with social workers emptied by "compassion fatigue" and sleep-deprived parents of eight-week-old twins. It is the expected consequence of pouring yourself out again and again and again.

Those of us who empty ourselves on behalf of others should learn to anticipate the drain. Know it is coming. Expect it. Don't be shocked when, after giving of yourself, you feel emptied and depleted. My friend, it's coming, so it's a good idea to decide what you are going to do about it before you get there.

AFTER THE MARATHON

A personal story about race recovery illustrates the importance of repairing our lives after a season of emotional exhaustion.

It was the day before the marathon. I dropped by the runners' expo to pick up my race number, commemorative T-shirt, and miscellaneous goodies the organizers toss into the race packets. Among these items was a small booklet containing a section titled "After the Marathon," which outlined what to do immediately after you cross the finish line of the 26.2-mile race.

Having completed prior marathons, I knew I wouldn't *want* to follow the booklet's recommendations. I needed to do what it said, but, having prior experience with the strange post-race cocktail of fatigue, soreness, and elation, I knew I wouldn't feel like doing the things prescribed. That's why I needed to commit to them before the race started.

What is healthy and healing is not always what we are drawn to when we're exhausted.

Over the years, I've encountered similar lists of those practices that speed recovery after a marathon. They include drinking

Gatorade or a similar sports drink. Now, if you've been downing this stuff intermittently for 26.2 miles, it's the last thing you want to ingest. Furthermore, you don't feel thirsty! You are also advised to eat something immediately, preferably something containing protein. You may not feel hungry or think you can even hold down food, but you're supposed to eat anyway—whether or not you feel like it.

Quite honestly, you want to collapse for a while, but instead you're supposed to peel off your wet clothing and put on something dry. This is more complicated than it might sound, because your leg muscles can be so tight that it's a challenge to merely reach your shoes and remove them. And that tightness is another thing—you need to stretch. Then, a short time after the marathon, you need—unbelievably—to walk or jog. Get your legs moving.

Oh, and then there's what *not* to do. Don't climb into a hot tub. I don't recall the exact science behind the concept, but your muscles need a plunge into cold water or an ice bath rather than a hot tub. Really?! Again, this isn't something you feel like doing at the time. But it's another practice that restores your body.

So, on several occasions after hobbling across a particular finish line near Lake Michigan, I've immediately gone through the post-race refreshment line to grab a banana, a bagel, and a bottle of dreaded sports drink. I've waded into the cold lake and plopped down, allowing the chilling waters to soothe my legs. Then I've changed into dry clothing and walked a couple of miles around town, preferably enjoying a hamburger somewhere along the way.

This is what I do when I am concerned with recovering as rapidly as possible. But what I actually want to do is avoid drinking or eating anything, lie around for a while, hang out in a hot tub, and then take a nap. The difference in these two approaches drastically affects how mobile I will be the next day.

The difference in recovery time is massive.

So let's talk about recovery. Not from marathon-length road races, but from the demands of our day-to-day lives and draining seasons.

SUNDAY AFTERNOONS

While fatigue affects us differently depending on our vocation and individual makeup, I resonate personally with what Charles Spurgeon divulged to his students about Sunday nights. "We feel as if life were completely washed out of us."

Usually, by Sunday afternoons, I'm emotionally spent from the weekend, with all its personal interactions and preaching three services. I generally feel emotionally, mentally, and psychologically drained. Like the post-marathon list, however, some things can restore me, but not necessarily things I desire to do.

I mention my own recovery process in the hope that you can apply something here, even if your calling and challenges are quite different from mine.

Following the drain of the weekend, I feel famished. I could eat half a large pizza and still feel unsatisfied. I'm confident this has more to do with emotional hunger than my need for food. If I allow myself to, I can lounge on the couch in a vegetative state, channel surfing for hours. If I can't find one great movie, I can toggle back and forth between three or four mediocre programs. Strangely, I feel I "deserve" this "downtime." The problem, though, is that these practices are not particularly restorative.

I'm fairly certain that overeating and watching hours of mindless TV do little to restore my energy and vitality for the coming week.

Fortunately, I've discovered a healthier Sunday afternoon routine. It often involves a small meal followed by a short nap. Then Chris and I routinely head out for a hike or leisurely bike ride. Nothing exhausting. Just going outside and getting our bodies moving. Returning from a walk or ride, I feel "fuller." I return home with far greater energy and a desire to engage with others more fully. Remember that self-care isn't selfish. You need to take care of yourself so you can take care of others.

Know that when you've emptied yourself, your heart grows hungry. When you are depleted, the temptation is to fill yourself with *anything*. I suspect many of us are drawn to overeating, excessive online shopping, mindless hours on social media, or pornography in these lonely hours. It fills the empty space for a moment, but ultimately steals more from us than we could imagine.

So decide what to do *before* you get there. Not unlike crossing the finish line of a marathon, determine in advance what restorative practices will speed your recovery.

Sometimes recovery involves inactivity. Sometimes it involves activity. You need to discern which events and practices genuinely restore you. Conversely, beware of those activities that consume vast amounts of time without refilling your tank. I'm thinking of the hours spent watching uninspiring TV or aimlessly surfing the internet all evening or playing video games into the early morning hours. Some of these activities are non-restorative, and we need to avoid them. They consume an enormous amount of time and don't refill an empty tank.

Figure out what these time wasters are for you and refuse to burn your life there.

LOOK AHEAD

Don't try to figure this out when you are exhausted. Discern in advance what practices restore you.

- Take a walk on a nature trail.
- Enjoy a classic movie.
- Sit beside a campfire or fireplace.
- Nap, in a hammock if possible.
- Thumb through a photo album of family pictures.
- Bike, hike, or boat.
- Read for pleasure.

Think of things that will fill *your* spirit. I'm deeply refreshed by sitting beside an evening fire.

And know that when you are really tired, you may not want to do any of these things. You will have to tell yourself, "This is healthy. This is filling. This restores." And then get up and do it. Others are counting on your energy and vitality. It's time to take care of yourself and speed along your recovery process.

I ask that our gracious Lord will fully restore *your* soul. As you pour yourself into others, may you discover those practices that bring life and vitality to your own heart. May you live, love, and lead from a heart that is fully alive.

REFLECTION

In Psalm 23:3, King David penned those beautiful lyrics, "He restores my soul" (NASB). As we close out Week Two, create two brief lists as you journey along the path to restoring your own soul.

1. List a few activities that can possibly refill your tank.

_____

_____

_____

_____

2. List a few activities that tend to be non-restorative time wasters.

_____

_____

_____

_____

WEEK THREE:

A HEALTHY HEART

GOOD TREES, GOOD FRUIT

Apple orchards flourish in our region. When our kids were small, each autumn included a pilgrimage to a local orchard, where delicious cider was pressed from the freshly picked fruit.

Good trees. Good fruit.

Jesus used this imagery when he pronounced, "Each tree is recognized by its own fruit" (Luke 6:44). He was alluding to the condition of the heart. A good heart produces blessing, while a nasty heart produces ruin.

The counsel of our Lord is this: If you desire to lead a life that blesses and enriches others, you need to pay attention to the condition of your heart. So in Week Three, let's talk about the health of your heart and how it makes all the difference.

DAY 11:

THE HIGHLIGHT REEL

I LOVE THE HIGHLIGHT CLIPS THEY SHOW ON *SportsCenter*. From an entire round of golf, one magnificent chip shot is selected—the ball arcing high, landing on the green, its backspin carrying it to within inches of the cup, the crowd erupting with spirited applause. The highlight reel speeds us to the fingertip catch in the corner of the end zone, the outfielder's perfectly timed leap to steal a home run, or the monster slam dunk in the NBA playoffs. The beauty of the highlight clip is that it cuts out the tedium, speeding us to a singular moment of awe.

But here's what generally doesn't make the highlight reel. A single to center field. A precision pass leading to a routine layup. A well-executed running play for a five-yard gain. We are unawed by the ordinary.

Something else doesn't make the *SportsCenter* highlight reel: the disciplined work required to make such routine plays look, well, routine. Stretching. Running laps. Hours spent in the weight room or practicing free throws in a gym, with no cheering fans and no applause. We love the highlight reel but are understandably bored by the quiet diligence that makes the highlights possible. This is one of the challenges of the Ant Power we talked about on Day 2. While the results of faithful discipline may be impressive, the actual tasks feel—and look—mundane, repetitive, and boring.

HEROICS IN THE BIBLE

This propensity to skip ahead to the action shots is true when we open our Bibles as well. We are drawn to those dynamic moments when courageous leaders perform heroically. Young David, equipped with an arsenal of a sling and five stones, squares off against the warrior Goliath. From Mount Carmel, Elijah challenges a wayward people, literally praying down fire from heaven. The prophet Daniel faces a pit of lions rather than turn his back on his God.

In these monumental stories, the faithful display their loyalty in climactic altercations. Images of these encounters filled the pages of my Sunday school papers when I was a child and formed my earliest impressions of what it meant to follow God.

But dig deeper. These pivotal events usually occur within a slow, steady, relatively uneventful stream of faithful living. Before David met Goliath, he was quietly guarding his family's flock of sheep. Elijah's confrontation with the prophets of Baal occurs after two years spent in seclusion—and immediately prior to an exhausted meltdown. And the famous story of Daniel and the den of lions? That transpires near the end of his journey—the apex of a lifetime of integrity, built on a foundation of persistent daily prayer.

It has taken me a long time to realize that these climactic, heroic events that form the biblical highlight reel are surrounded by lengthy seasons of simple, non-spectacular faithfulness. Extraordinary moments emerge from ordinary faithfulness.

THE QUIET JESUS

Even the ministry of Jesus had its own quiet, non-astounding moments. As you read the Gospels (Matthew, Mark, Luke, and John), notice what Jesus is doing *between* his stunning miracles. These quiet moments are easily missed and largely ignored.

I noticed this when reading through the life of Jesus not long ago. I began scouring his story for normality. I looked for mundane, faithful, run-of-the-mill ministry moments. They were everywhere.

I noticed that the astonishing events in Jesus's ministry—the highlight reel—occurred when he was engaged in comparatively uneventful routine. Many of the healings and memorable conversations took place while he was going about ordinary work—like faithfully teaching or praying or having dinner at someone's house. This came as a new insight because I tended to view Jesus as bounding from one miracle to the next. What I gained was new appreciation for the norm. Jesus's moments of profound power were unleashed in the midst of everyday faithfulness.

In a story we will return to on Day 15, we see Jesus teaching in the synagogue in Capernaum. As he teaches, his sermon is interrupted by the screams of a man plagued by demonic influence. Stunning the congregation, Jesus delivers the man from this dark oppression. The setting for this paranormal event? Jesus is going about the very normal business of teaching in a Sabbath synagogue service.

A short time later, while Jesus is in a house teaching, four guys chop a hole in the roof and lower their paralyzed buddy down to Jesus. The story is remarkable. The friends show initiative, someone gets their roof dismantled, and the guy who is carried in later skips out. But notice the setting for this riveting story. Jesus sits in a house teaching. The extraordinary miracle occurs as he's faithfully going about his ordinary business.

And what about the famous story of Peter obediently rowing out into the lake after a sleepless night of unsuccessful fishing? His boat is swamped by a spectacular catch of fish. Miraculous! And before the miracle? Jesus sits in Peter's boat, teaching the people who listen from the shore.

Don't miss the routine parts. The parts where Jesus is going about his business in faithful obedience to his Father. Take time to absorb the ordinary moments that don't make the highlight reel.

Watch Jesus pray. The following sentences are story openers drawing us to his commitment to isolated periods of prayer (emphasis mine).

> *Once when* Jesus was praying *in private and his disciples were with him . . . (Luke 9:18)*
>
> *Jesus . . . took Peter, John and James with him and went up onto a mountain* to pray. *(Luke 9:28)*
>
> *One day* Jesus was praying *in a certain place. (Luke 11:1)*

These three lines illustrate Jesus's practice of removing himself from the noise of the crowds to talk to his Father. He did this again and again. Not exactly highlight reel material. Ah, but the three events that roll out of these quiet moments are monumental—Peter's great confession: "You are the Christ, the

Son of the living God" (Matt. 16:16 NASB); the transfiguration; and Jesus's giving us the Lord's Prayer.

The spectacular moments emerge in settings of ordinary, redundant faithfulness. I find this reassuring, for much of the faithful life isn't all that exciting.

We get up and go to work. We send our kids off to school. We care for an elderly parent. We encourage coworkers and serve customers. We sit on our church board or clean the church building. We pray over the sick and discouraged. We faithfully teach a Sunday school class or lead a Bible study. It's not the stuff likely to make the highlight reel. But these small acts of faithfulness, repeated over and over, are important. They count. This is the legacy of faithful living.

And sometimes, in a season of faithfulness, the power of God breaks through in remarkable ways. Giants tumble, fire falls, and the mouths of lions are shut. Sins are forgiven, destructive habits are broken, and alienated families are restored.

Over the next three days, we will explore the value of using a journal to meet with God daily. Sitting with an open notebook and inviting God into our day doesn't exactly look like material for the highlight reel. But it can be a powerful tool in cultivating and maintaining a healthy heart.

I challenge you to remain faithful with the small stuff and trust God to work miracles in the midst of the mundane. Stretch. Run your laps. Practice your free throws. Trust God to provide the highlights.

REFLECTION

What are some of the tasks you do quietly and diligently that wouldn't make the highlight reel? Write them down here and know that Jesus celebrates every one of your faithful actions.

_____

_____

_____

_____

DAY 12:

A DIALOGUE WITH YOUR SOUL

STRETCHING. LAPS. FREE THROWS. THE ORDINARY activity that makes a highlight reel possible. Over the next three days, we'll be exploring an exercise that I've come to depend on for the maintenance of a healthy heart: the quiet practice of journaling.

I journal faithfully. Not every single day, but several times a week. I don't practice this discipline because I enjoy it. I use a journal because I pray badly without one.

Heroes of intercessory prayer may find that time flies as they communicate with the Father, uttering their thanksgiving and petitions with unbroken flow and focus for extended periods of time. If that describes you, what I am about to say could feel alien or just plain wrong.

The truth of the matter is that I have trouble concentrating when I pray. Often, without the aid of pen and paper, my prayers lose their focus. My mind can wander even when I'm conversing with someone and looking directly at them. It's worse when I'm talking to Someone I can't see (which is precisely what prayer is). I start out praying about something, then I'm thinking about someone else, then I'm texting that someone. Or making a notation on my to-do list. Or pouring myself a cup of coffee. Or putting frozen waffles in the toaster. And suddenly I'm thinking, "Wait a minute! Did I say amen?"

This is why I journal.

Journaling allows me to focus my random thoughts and wandering mind into articulate, coherent sentences. On days when I journal, I quiet myself in the morning to express thanks to my Lord by itemizing elements of my life for which I am deeply grateful. I write about the beauty of the day—falling snow, sweet rain, or changing leaves—thanking my Creator for the glory that surrounds me. Sometimes I scribble urgent prayers, asking for God's filling and grace in the conflicts, challenges, and decisions I face. And I've gotten into the habit of adding a line or two each day that simply recalls who I am. It's the way I talk to God. It's also the way I record what I hear from God.

Journaling faithfully develops the foundation of my life—the part that lies below the surface. The crucial part nobody sees. Writing in my journal is a way for me to build my private life so my public life can hold up under the storms, stress, and pressure that come my way.

As Gordon MacDonald articulated, "A journal is a dialogue with my soul."[1] Through the medium of my journal, I keep track of my ups and downs, my achievements and failures, my frustrations, insights, and disappointments. I journal because it's good for my heart.

You may be thinking, "But, Jeff, I'm not a writer. If I sat down with a pen and paper, I wouldn't know what to write."

I understand. The thought of engaging in prayer of any sort can leave a person feeling overwhelmed or underqualified. While I don't know what will work for you, I want to share three practices, both here and in the next couple of chapters, that have been exceedingly helpful in my daily journey.

PRACTICE 1: FILLING

Daily, I plant myself in a chair in a quiet corner, open my journal, and ask myself the simple question, "Jeff, how's your heart?"

Many days I find my heart is at peace, brimming with gratitude, joy, and hope. And some days I detect latent anxiety, pent-up resentment, or an undercurrent of anger. I desire to treat people well, but if I detect dark threads crisscrossing my spirit, I want to get my heart straight before I plow into my day so I don't inflict myself on those who have the misfortune of encountering me. I need Jesus very badly, and reflecting on the condition of my heart is a necessary first step.

Wise King Solomon penned this proverb prioritizing heart protection: "Above all else, guard your heart, for everything you do flows from it" (Prov. 4:23).

Reflect for a moment on that statement. Everything you do—every response, every reaction, every decision—flows from a healthy or unhealthy heart.

Listen to the clarity with which Jesus spoke about the heart as he addressed curious crowds in Galilee: "A good man brings good things out of the good stored up in his heart, and an evil man brings evil things out of the evil stored up in his heart. For the mouth speaks what the heart is full of" (Luke 6:45).

We speak from the heart. You may have heard someone described as "wearing her heart on her sleeve." Actually, we all wear our hearts on our *lips*. If I blaze into my day with resentful, anxious, impatient, or angry words, I can be sure of one thing: I don't just have a "word problem"; I have a "heart problem."

I need to talk these things over with God.

Even though the practice might not come easily, we could all benefit from journaling on a regular basis to honestly monitor the condition of our hearts. Simply penning the words, "How's my heart today?" at the top of the page and letting our thoughts flow can be a huge step in inviting God into the day.

When I'm journaling, I find it helpful to ask, "Who or what is troubling me? What am I afraid of? Am I anxious about an appointment, a conversation, or decision? Am I upset about someone or a situation I'm dreading?"

In examining the condition of my heart, I become aware of my daily need for God's filling. I desperately need my Lord if I am to approach situations with kindness, courage, and wisdom. I don't pray only because I want to pray; I also pray because of my propensity to be impatient, anxious, and petty, and because I desperately need God's provision in my life.

I ask God to meet me in this unsettled space and provide the resources I need to move into my day with a spirit free to serve. I believe our Lord is pleased to provide what we need when we humble ourselves and ask for his strength.

I often review the traits listed in Galatians 5:22–23, where Paul describes the fruit of the Spirit. I name them one by one: Love. Joy. Peace. Forbearance. Kindness. Goodness. Faithfulness. Gentleness. Self-control.

This is not "The fruit of Jeff." This is the fruit of God's Spirit. This is the harvest God desires to grow in my life when I humbly allow him to work. It requires the awareness that I am lost without his daily work in my heart and that I am in continual need. With journal open and pen in hand, I ask the Lord to generously provide everything I need to love and serve people well.

God is eager to provide what you could never pull off on your own. He wants to fill you and empower you with himself.

How might your day change if you asked the Holy Spirit to grant you a measure of gentleness when your patience is running thin or for peace to replace your runaway anxiety? What if you pleaded with God to give you the ability to love someone you've been finding particularly annoying, or to bring joy in the middle of a disruptive mess?

I don't know what specific practices will best equip you to move into your day with grace, but I have found that this particular habit empowers me to live and serve out of a more joyful, gracious spirit. The practice of asking for God's daily filling redirects my heart, exposing and correcting dark patterns that could prove lethal if left unaltered.

Keep one thing in mind, though. None of this is a quick fix to a powerful life. It's all about small, faithful steps compounded over time. Even in prayer and journaling, it pays to think small.

REFLECTION

Respond to the question, "How's your heart?" Where do you need God's fresh filling in your life today?

_____

_____

_____

DAY 13:

THE POWER OF A THANKFUL HEART

I'M GRATEFUL TODAY.

I'm grateful for the steaks and asparagus we grilled last night in our backyard and for the warm May temperatures in which to enjoy our meal outdoors. I'm thankful that the color green dominates the landscape, displacing the drab colors of our long Michigan winter. I'm grateful for my bike and the laughter and company of the guys I rode with Thursday evening. And I'm thankful today for the good news we received that a beloved family member, long hospitalized, has improved enough to return home soon.

Today I give thanks to God, expressing gratitude for these gifts and others too numerous to relate.

Expressing gratitude may seem like a small thing. But the person you are becoming is largely determined by the repetition of small things. The practice of offering thanks cultivates the heart a day at a time. With gratitude, it pays to think small.

What are you thankful for today? Take a moment to think about it. A friend? A family member? A delicious meal? Birds outside your window? A car that starts consistently? For what are you grateful?

PRACTICE 2: GRATITUDE

I use my journal to express gratitude to God. I began this practice because I live a truly blessed existence and I don't want to rush from day to day, oblivious to the gifts that bombard my life. I deeply desire to become a person marked by gratitude. I don't want to take God's gifts for granted, so each day I jot down three things for which I am grateful. This gratitude exercise awakens my heart to the goodness that surrounds me.

Most of the things I list are simple pleasures of life that can easily go undetected. Scrambled eggs. Heat in our home. Dessert with friends. The joy of hanging out with my adult children. Treasured time spent playing with a grandchild.

I attempt to be specific, not listing "shelter, clothing, and food," but precise gratitude for my Chaco sandals, the macaroni and cheese we enjoyed for dinner last night, or the freedom of a schedule that allows us to drive to Chicago to visit our daughter, Sarah, and her husband, Matt.

I try not to repeat myself in my gratitude exercise but instead to identify fresh blessings that have escaped my notice. I could easily get stuck mentioning the same things again and again, so I scan my life to identify new expressions of God's kindness.

And I know this: If I can't identify three things for which I am grateful, I may have grown numb or blind to God's goodness.

ANXIETY AND GRATITUDE

Some seasons of life leave us feeling body-slammed. In these times, gratitude to God aids our survival. When we're immersed in grief or traveling through a debilitating illness, the power of gratitude can lift our soul and awaken us to God's goodness that falls like rain all around us. It can prove to be a powerful tool in finding joy in a season of trial.

The firm foundation of gratitude can stabilize us in the storm, keeping us grounded in the knowledge of God's gracious provision.

Anxiety. Worry. Fear. Thieves that rob us of joy and peace. Anxiety about tomorrow can steal the enjoyment of today.

To Christians in northern Greece, the apostle Paul offered this encouragement:

Do not be anxious about anything, but in every situation, by prayer and petition, with thanksgiving, present your requests to God. And the peace of God, which transcends all understanding, will guard your hearts and your minds in Christ Jesus. (Phil. 4:6–7)

I am comforted and challenged when I recall that these words were written by an inmate. The letter to the Philippians is a "prison epistle"—a letter penned by Paul while he was incarcerated, most likely in Rome. Chained to a Roman guard and facing an uncertain future, he wrote, "Do not be anxious about anything."

Paul encouraged us to refuse to cave in to a life of suffocating anxiety. Instead, we are to pour out our requests before God.

And God's peace will protect our lives, replacing the worry that holds us hostage.

Focus with me on two words that often get overlooked in this beautiful passage: "*with thanksgiving*, present your requests to God."

Our urgent requests are to be accompanied by offerings of thanks. When plagued by difficulty and overrun with challenges, a remedy for peace involves gratitude. As you pray, mention to God all that is going wrong. But also offer thanks for the blessings that flood your life. Thankfulness is an enemy of anxiety. They are incompatible roommates.

I did not adopt this practice because I am the gold standard for gratitude. I itemize these expressions of grace because I am fearful of taking things for granted. I am at risk of receiving a thousand gifts that flow from the Giver and failing to recognize them. I journal my gratitude in an attempt to rescue my soul from the onslaught of anxiety, complaint, and envy. I journal my gratitude because of the man I desire to become.

As we recognize the blessings—both great and small—that flood our lives every day, we will experience the joy God intended for us. That is the power of a thankful heart.

REFLECTION

How could your perspective on life change if you made it a practice to chronicle your gratitude? Pause for a moment right now and express gratitude for three specific blessings in your life.

Dear Lord, today I am grateful for:

* _____

* _____

* _____

DAY 14:

REMEMBERING WHO YOU ARE

WHO ARE YOU? AT A BASIC LEVEL, THE QUESTION CAN be answered by giving your name: "I'm Jeff."

But identity runs deeper than a name. It expands to include our relationship to family members—our role as husband or wife, child or parent. So someone pointing across the room at me might accurately say, "That's Chris's husband," or "He's Andrew's dad."

This is why we can find ourselves in an identity crisis if recently divorced or widowed or if we lose a parent or a child. Part of who we are is in relationship to someone else, and that has been stripped away.

Our profession generally gets tossed into the identity mix. I'm a student, a plumber, a money manager, an insurance agent, a stay-at-home parent, an artist, a chef.

We also tend to draw our identity from those achievements and failures that seem to mark our lives.

So. Who are you? What is the most true thing about who

you are? And why does identity matter in cultivating a healthy heart—a heart from which we can serve and love others with longevity?

I have found that pausing each day to remember my identity as God's treasured son restores something in me. Recalling my identity as one deeply loved by the Father empowers me to love and serve from a space of security and significance.

PRACTICE 3: IDENTITY

The third daily practice I cling to deals with my identity. I sign off almost every journal entry with the phrase, *This is Jeff, your beloved son.*

I don't do this to remind God who I am. I do this to remind *me* who I am—an adopted child of the Creator of the planet.

In his letter to Jesus's followers living in and around Ephesus, the apostle Paul penned these words: "In love he predestined us for adoption to sonship through Jesus Christ, in accordance with his pleasure and will" (Eph. 1:4–5).

Before he told the believers to do anything, Paul reminded them that they were God's adopted kids.

We are the beloved sons and daughters of God. We are wanted, adored, treasured. Our Father so desired to bring us into his family that he gave of himself—his own Son—to rescue us and bring us home.

That's why I write, *This is Jeff, your beloved son.*

It's the most true thing about who I am. And it's the one thing that can never be stripped away.

This practice—reminding ourselves who we truly are—is so

crucial because we attempt to find our core identity from so many other sources: other people, a career, ministry success, or objects we acquire. While the quiet voice of God whispers that we are deeply loved, we continue to search for an alternative. We move from person to person or event to event, trying to satisfy our inner craving for significance. Henri Nouwen wrote:

> Aren't you, like me, hoping that some person, thing, or event will come along to give you that final feeling of inner well-being you desire? Don't you often hope: "May this book, idea, course, trip, job, country, or relationship fulfill my deepest desire."[1]

But even if we obtain the objects we pursue, they prove feeble and unreliable substitutes for the stable identity that is ours when we come to know Jesus. Our deepest longings are only fully met in our identity as God's treasured and cherished children.

It might be difficult for you to comprehend, but I want you to understand that you are a beloved son or daughter. Take a moment to either write it out or say it out loud:

This is _____, *your beloved child.*

I challenge you to write this phrase in your journal day after day, week after week, to remember that your primary identity is not formed by adding up your accomplishments. Neither is it found in the sum of your failures. Your fundamental identity is found in your adoption. He picked you out. He picked you up. He brought you home.

Often it takes years—or even a lifetime—to truly believe

that we are deeply loved. Through recalling our identity, we take small steps toward the waiting Father, whose arms await his beloved kids.

The Creator adopted me as his son. He loves me, enjoys me, and desires to form me into the person he created me to be. I am his. Yet I am prone to find my identity in work, or stuff, or popularity rating. So I remind myself again and again. I am his.

I write it out, word for word. *This is Jeff, the son you love.*

WHAT'S THE POINT?

Your goal shouldn't be to fill your journal with words. The journal is only a tool. For me, the journal is a vehicle to (1) ask for daily filling, (2) express gratitude, and (3) recall my core identity. I journal to get my heart right and to keep it right. This may seem a small thing, but life is built from small steps, taken repeatedly, in the holy direction.

A foundation is not built in a day. A good foundation takes time and focus. It is formed by one scribbled prayer at a time. Over the years, that base will grow strong enough to support a life well lived.

REFLECTION

If you haven't already started a journaling practice, begin right now. Use this space to ask God for his daily filling, to express your gratitude, and to recall your core identity as his beloved child.

_____

_____

_____

_____

_____

DAY 15:

YOU CAN'T DO IT ALL

IN NEED OF INSPIRATION AND REFRESHED VISION, I attended a conference in downtown Chicago. A parade of gifted communicators ascended the steps of the stage and spoke passionately of brokenness in the world. Each one urged us to become part of the solution, to bring healing and restoration to the brokenness.

The presenters shared stories and statistics that highlighted the need for their ministries. One spoke of the plight of young men without dads and the desperate need for stable mentors to fill the role of father figures. Another shared about a ministry to prison inmates, reminding the audience of Jesus's words in Matthew 25:36: "I was in prison and you came to visit me."

Then came a compelling challenge for churches to embrace their alienated artists by exploring more creative expressions of worship. There was also a session unveiling the horror of sex trafficking and the immediate response required of any conscientious believer, a strong appeal to sponsor impoverished children in developing countries, and a plea to provide clean drinking water in under-resourced parts of the globe.

By the end of the first day, my heart was tired. Instead of a fresh infusion of vision, I found myself beginning to shut down. As the presentations compounded, with their corresponding calls to action, I began to grow numb. The overload wasn't caused by any single speaker but by the weight of their collective voice.

Were the needs they spoke of real? Yes, very much so. Then why the emotional shutdown? Because the sum of all the world's brokenness is so much greater than my ability to engage it, much less solve it.

The unspoken implication was that any caring ministry— any church worth its salt—would devote itself to these critical causes. All of them. Nobody actually verbalized it, but the message seemed to be, "How can you claim to love Jesus and not be serving the people *we're* committed to serve?"

THE MORNING JESUS DISAPPEARED

You may be protesting, "Yeah, but didn't Jesus heal the sick and feed the hungry?"

Yes. He did.

He healed *some* of the sick and fed *some* of the hungry. But not even Jesus tried to do it all at once.

He made choices—sometimes agonizing choices—about how to invest his time and energy. We find him making one of these choices near the beginning of his ministry.

Early one Sunday, as a large, needy crowd gathered, his disciples awakened to discover him missing.

The day before Jesus's disappearance is extraordinary. That

Saturday, Jesus teaches powerfully in the synagogue service in Capernaum. (This is the service we mentioned briefly on Day 11.) His sermon is interrupted by the shouts of a man afflicted by a demon. Jesus orders the demon to exit its human host, and the man thrashes as the demon departs with a screech. The people are stunned. This is not your run-of-the-mill synagogue service. The crowd marvels that this young rabbi holds authority over demonic powers. "Immediately the news about Him spread everywhere into all the surrounding district of Galilee" (Mark 1:28 NASB).

Jesus's reputation skyrockets. But this hallmark day isn't over.

Jesus leaves the synagogue and heads to the home of Andrew and Simon (also called Peter). Simon's mother-in-law lies sick in bed, plagued by a fever. Jesus heals her, and news of his power now spreads faster and farther.

Not only can he drive out evil spirits, but Jesus also has authority over illness.

Now the sick and those haunted by demons are carried to the home where Jesus ministers until long after sunset.

Finally, Jesus and his friends call it a night. They will return to the sick and distraught the next day. But the following morning, the disciples awaken to discover they have a big problem. The star attraction is missing. Gone. Jesus has disappeared. But to where, and why?

Mark tells us. "Very early in the morning, while it was still dark, Jesus got up, left the house and went off to a solitary place, where he prayed" (Mark 1:35).

Before daybreak, Jesus slips away to a place of solitude to pray. This isn't the only time he did this. Luke informs us, "Jesus often withdrew to lonely places and prayed" (Luke 5:16). In the quiet morning solitude, Jesus goes away and hides to seek direction and clarity. Away from the traffic and the noise, away from the crowds and their demands, Jesus finds a quiet space to talk with his Father.

But while Jesus is having his quiet time, the disciples awaken to the needs of the world. I sense something of a panic as the crowd gathers, demanding an audience with Jesus. Unable to find him, the disciples form a search party and scour the area to seek for the truant healer.

When they finally find him, Jesus's reaction is totally unexpected. "Let us go somewhere else—to the nearby villages—so I can preach there also. That is why I have come" (Mark 1:38).

At this stage of his ministry, he experiences a conflict between his teaching ministry and his healing ministry. In this instance, teaching wins out over healing.

This may tweak your image of Jesus. In this season, he is not the gentle healer traveling from village to village, looking for people to restore to health. He is the traveling teacher followed by a pack of people seeking healing.

MISSION CLARITY

And so it was, early one morning, in the midst of rocketing popularity, Jesus found a quiet place—away from the crowds and their demands—to ask his Father for direction. In solitude, Jesus detected his primary mission for this season of his ministry. He took action to prevent his healing ministry from eclipsing his teaching ministry. Jesus knew why he had come and what he had been called to do.

If Jesus—God in human skin—found it necessary to escape

the noise and commune with his Father, how much more do we need to find a quiet place to spend time with our Father?

People yell.

God often whispers.

We have to quiet ourselves to hear his voice.

The outcome of Jesus's early morning getaway was clarity of vision and mission. It gave him certainty to announce, "Let us go somewhere else—to the nearby villages—so I can preach there also. That is why I have come."

Do you realize the freedom this story brings? Jesus's statement liberates us to discern our calling in each season of life. To both say yes and no.

Our challenge is to consistently separate ourselves from the noise, the demands, and the traffic—to quiet ourselves to hear the voice of the Father. In stillness we discern those needs he is calling *us* to meet and which heartbreaking needs he will call *others* to meet.

You can't do everything. And you shouldn't.

Knowing this frees us to focus on what we can and should do. It grants clarity of purpose.

NOBODY DOES EVERYTHING

As I reflect back on the emotional drain of the conference in downtown Chicago, I think the pressure many of us in attendance felt stemmed from an implied *and* rather than a liberating *or*.

Now, I might be going out on a limb here, but I'm guessing that none of the conference speakers excelled at *everything* that was presented at the conference. The church pouring massive energy into creative worship experiences might not be conducting a transformational prison ministry. And the church rallying its resources around digging wells and sponsoring impoverished children might not be modeling artistic genius or running a flagship mentoring program.

Nobody does it all. Or at least not for long.

My friend, serving others with passion and excellence requires heart-focus. For Jesus, this was reaffirmed when he disappeared to be with his Father. When we quiet ourselves to hear his voice, we are more likely to discern our mission for a given season.

MISSION ACCOMPLISHED

The night Jesus was arrested, hours before the crucifixion, he was able to pray, "I have brought you glory on earth *by finishing the work you gave me to do*" (John 17:4, emphasis mine).

Not every disabled person could walk, and not all the blind could see. But Jesus faithfully completed the work his Father assigned to him. He was faithful but not frantic. Not even Jesus attempted to serve everyone in every way.

Realizing that you can't do it all *can* liberate you to hear the voice of the Father and respond to his unique calling upon your life. It can also deliver you from guilt imposed by not doing it all.

As a young pastor I received some solid advice: "There is never enough time to do everything you want to do, but there is always enough time to do the work God is calling you to do."

REFLECTION

Are you chronically overcommitted and still feel like you aren't doing enough? I urge you to take ten minutes to answer a couple of questions. Find a quiet place to sit and, after several minutes of silence, respond to these two questions.

1. In this season of my life, what is one crucial opportunity I fully believe is from God—something I need to say yes to? This may be a person in whom you are investing, a task that needs to be completed, or an ongoing ministry opportunity.

   _____

   _____

   _____

2. In this season of my life, what is an opportunity to which I need to say no? It may be a wonderful calling for another person or another season, but for now, it will only pull me away from the other responsibilities God is calling me to fulfill.

   _____

   _____

   _____

WEEK FOUR:

LIFE-GIVING RELATIONSHIPS

WHILE I WAS TRAVELING IN ZAMBIA NOT LONG AGO, a pastor reminded me of this famous African proverb:

> If you want to go fast, travel alone.
> If you want to go far, travel together.

This well-known couplet suggests that a lengthy journey is best shared with others. Faithfulness is an endurance race and is most successful when traveled in the company of those who encourage our steady forward movement.

To this point, much of our conversation about consistency

and perseverance could be applied on an individual basis. Now, in Week Four, let's turn our attention to the strength we find through the companionship of others and the strength they may find through our companionship.

DAY 16:

THE GIFT OF
LONG-TERM FRIENDS

I SIT IN AN OVERSTUFFED CHAIR LOOKING OUT OVER Lake Michigan. The floor-to-ceiling windows across the room frame a magnificent picture of the water. The whipping November wind of yesterday has died down a bit, and today the waves roll gently onto the shore.

Later this morning, we will gather around the dining room table to study segments of Luke's gospel. But in these early hours, the lake house is quiet. We rise when we feel like it, make coffee, sit in various parts of the house, read, write, and reflect.

The four of us meet here twice a year—spring and fall. We take a breather from the churches we lead and gather at this cottage to repair and replenish our lives. It's not just the break from church life that is refilling, but the company of brothers who build into each other's lives. We've met like this for more than twenty years. When we initiated our twice-yearly retreats, my children were preschoolers. Now I am a grandfather. That's a long time.

The makeup of the group changed a bit in the early years as guys moved in and out of the region and we used a variety of cottages. But for the last ten or so years the four of us have been meeting in this beloved lake house.

We come together to invest in each other but also in ourselves.

These guys know me. They see both my hidden potential and the blind spots that could wreck me. They know my capabilities and my liabilities. They knew me when my church was small and struggling to get off the ground. They love me but are utterly unimpressed with any achievements with which I may be credited. They know me for who I am and not necessarily for anything I have accomplished. This is the kind of knowledge that comes only with time.

We have the privilege of pastoring each other. We are better men for being in each other's lives.

Carlton flies in from San Diego. I drive less than an hour to the lake house. He usually flies through the night to be here. He remains part of our group, though it is not convenient or inexpensive. It is a costly friendship for him, but well worth it.

When we return to our respective cities, he and I stay in touch through regular Monday phone conversations. "How did your weekend go? Are you encouraged or discouraged? What new opportunities or disappointments have invaded your life?" Carlton routinely inquires about the health of my marriage, the spiritual lives of my children, and whether I am experiencing satisfying moments with God.

Would I still be in ministry without these friendships? Probably. Would I be serving out of a healthy, joy-filled, authentic space? Possibly not.

If you are fully engaged, life is draining. You constantly pour yourself into people. This persistent pouring can leave you spent and depleted. You need refilling and recharging.

It's good to know I am not traveling alone. I draw strength from these guys at the lake and, I trust, they draw strength from me. These relationships are foundational. We dive into that area below the surface that few people see. Withdrawing from the public eye empowers us to serve more faithfully when we are back in the public eye. Our private commitments empower our public commitments.

I wish everyone had such an enduring band of friends.

THE JOURNEY TOGETHER

In Ecclesiastes, King Solomon warned of the danger of traveling alone and pointed out the advantage of banding together for the journey. In his poem advocating camaraderie, he advises, "Two are better than one" (Eccl. 4:9). He then draws upon various travel scenarios where companionship can prove lifesaving.

> *If either of them falls down,*
> *one can help the other up.*
> *But pity anyone who falls*
> *and has no one to help them up.*
> *Also, if two lie down together, they will keep warm.*
> *But how can one keep warm alone?*
> *Though one may be overpowered,*
> *two can defend themselves. (Eccl. 4:10–12)*

Solomon describes a world that is neither safe nor sure. We fall, we get caught in the cold, and we come under attack. You cannot predict when these calamities will strike. You don't know when you will trip, or shiver in the cold, or be threatened with a mugging. The wise king's advice? "Don't travel alone." When we travel together, we can pick each other up, share warmth, and protect each other. But if we travel life alone . . . well, good luck.

Don't wait till the bottom drops out of your life before you scramble to identify the friends who can bolster you. The friendships we build when nothing is going wrong sustain us when everything is going wrong. Your commitment to travel with someone when you are sure-footed, warm, and secure builds the relationship for the day you trip, or shiver, or find yourself unexpectedly under siege.

ROPE

To add even more reinforcement to his challenge, King Solomon added a rope metaphor to his encouragement. "A cord of three strands is not quickly broken" (Eccl. 4:12).

The image here is of a rope crafted from multiple strands. The rope is strong, enduring pressure without snapping. Each strand is essential to the strength of the cord. The strands are twisted and woven together, intertwining to create a powerful bond.

Alone, I am string. Together, we are rope. It's a great image of enduring friendships.

And that is why I am eager to be back at the lake house, to gather as we have for twenty years. Our lives are intertwined. Together, we are strong.

These kinds of friendships take time. We build them over cups of coffee, texts or emails asking how it's going, routine phone calls, and unrushed meals. These relationships are generally the product of years and not weeks. Over time, we band together for strength.

If you want to finish well, devote your heart and schedule to life-sustaining friendships. If you aspire to lead and serve for decades, band together with others. Enjoy the journey together.

REFLECTION

Are you connected to friends you can call upon when life gets difficult? Who can you reach out to if you find yourself trapped, confused, or dejected? Take a moment to list them by name.

* _____
* _____
* _____
* _____

If you were unable to list the names of those whom you might call upon in a season of challenge, then list individuals with whom you could potentially build life-giving friendships. Write down those with whom you could invest time and trust, those who could become potential traveling companions and friends with whom to share the journey.

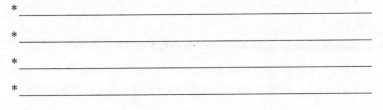

* _____
* _____
* _____
* _____

DAY 17:

THE CIRCLE

ARON RALSTON WAS HIKING ALONE. AND NOBODY knew where he was.

Aron's harrowing story is chronicled in his book *Between a Rock and a Hard Place,* which inspired the 2010 movie *127 Hours.* In April 2003, Ralston was hiking in Canyonlands National Park in Utah when an 800-pound rock dislodged and pinned his arm against the canyon wall. Ralston was trapped for more than five days, slowly dying of dehydration. Finally, he freed himself by amputating his right forearm with the dull pocketknife of his multi-tool.

As I read of Ralston's life-threatening experience in *National Geographic Adventure,*[1] I was struck by a statement describing the reason for his traumatic ordeal: "Ralston had not informed anyone of his hiking plans, so no one would have been searching for him."

He was hiking alone, and nobody knew where he was.

Even though we might not be literally trapped in a canyon or lost in the woods, many of us *are* hiking alone. And hiking alone can be risky. Maybe nobody knows where we are. Perhaps we are struggling in isolation, dying a day at a time. Or we've cut ourselves off from those who could help. We may even have withdrawn from community, cocooning when we are in greatest need of friendship.

Building a strong private world, a foundation for our lives, includes cultivating a circle of trusted friends. Often we remain trapped because we hike alone. And nobody knows where we are.

THE WEDNESDAY CIRCLE

The five of us gathered for years, meeting early Wednesday mornings in one of our offices or occasionally at a restaurant. I don't recall any neatly crafted mission statement, but the point was fairly clear—we met to encourage one another to become better husbands, better dads, better followers of Christ. We wanted to become better men and believed our odds of pulling this off greatly increased if we banded together rather than hike alone.

One particular morning, someone in the group looked across the circle and asked how I was doing. And I told the truth. I was terrible. I was tired and uninspired—trudging from week to week with little joy and decreased enthusiasm for serving my congregation. I was enduring the longest sustained stretch of depression I had ever experienced.

The emotional downswing had begun shortly after our congregation moved into a new building. The relocation represented a major achievement for a church that had struggled for years to merely get off the ground. After selling our former building and renting a high school for a couple of years, we'd successfully completed a multi-million-dollar construction project on sixty spacious acres.

This should have been a time of deep fulfillment over a job well done, but instead I was slogging through a swamp of discouragement. I use the word *depression* reluctantly, because I was not engulfed in total emotional darkness. It wasn't a clinical depression marked by the inability to function, but an extended season of the blues. A gray cloud hovered above my life for months.

An emotional dip generally follows the completion of any major project. In addition, occupying our new building prompted a surge in attendance, adding additional strain to our staff and volunteers. We were all tired. I should have seen the dip coming. But I didn't.

As we sat in the circle, I described the heaviness I carried. A disturbing feature of my condition was that I was no longer finding fulfillment in what I had consistently enjoyed during my first sixteen years in ministry—crafting sermons and delivering them to a responsive congregation. Sermon preparation had become a joyless chore, and I found myself exiting weekend services with little sense of satisfaction or fulfillment. My weekly regimen had become a lifeless grind. It wasn't fun anymore.

Feeling that something was terribly wrong, I scrutinized each weekend. Was I stuck in my depressive swamp or moving forward out of it? Was joy returning to my work, and if not, how and when would it return? What had I done to enter this fog, and what could I do to shake it?

WISE COUNSEL

The guys in the small circle listened without interrupting. When I completed my rant, they sat there for a while, allowing silence to replace my noise. They were in no hurry to speak or recommend or fix.

While three of my friends in the circle attended other churches, Tim sat under my teaching each week. One of the guys asked him to weigh in. "Tim, is Jeff effective?" he asked. Tim responded that he believed my teaching ministry was highly effective, that he had heard several attendees comment recently that my messages had been helpful and made an impact. He judged that, regardless of what I might be experiencing, my effectiveness had not plummeted.

A long pause followed, and then Kurt spoke. "Jeff, if people are learning and growing, does it really matter what *you* are getting out of the experience?"

Ugh.

Then more silence, followed by a life-giving suggestion. "What if God is calling you to a season of faithfulness when you don't receive much gratification in return? What if that is your assignment right now—just to be faithful?"

I distinctly remember crossing the parking lot that morning and driving home feeling like a free man. The idea was liberating. "I don't have to enjoy this right now," I thought. "Maybe my joy will return quickly and maybe it won't, but that's not my job." This liberation was accompanied by resolve, and that's when another powerful thought ensued. "For the time being, I yield my right to enjoy the process. I commit to bring my full self to my work every week, whether or not I experience satisfaction. For this next stretch,

I yield my right to personal fulfillment." And with that vow, I let go of the weekly scrutiny. I resolved to show up and serve and allow God to restore my emotional satisfaction when he chose to.

And something happened.

Soon I began to enjoy the process once again. When I relinquished my right to fulfillment, I began to taste it. Soon after that Wednesday morning gathering, I emerged from the darkness.

Looking back, I believe I had burrowed deeper and deeper into introspection, becoming obsessed with *my* experience, *my* fulfillment, and *my* right to happiness. I had unintentionally spiraled downward into a vortex of self-absorption.

HIKING TOGETHER

Now, I don't suggest that my experience is a blanket fix for discouragement or depression. Life is far too messy and mysterious for a one-size-fits-all remedy. But the interaction with my circle of committed friends showed me the path out of the most prolonged season of discouragement in my professional life.

Depression is overcome in a variety of ways, and I don't claim to be an expert on it. One thing I do know is that depression, like most other struggles, should not be tackled alone. Like anything, it is best fought with the support of loving friends—a circle that hangs together for the long haul.

I didn't find my way out alone. I had help. I was committed— for years—to a group of guys who watched over one another's lives. We made it our business to ask, "Where are you? How is your heart? What is the condition of your soul?"

I exited my canyon of discouragement, whole and encouraged,

in the company of friends. I was not hiking alone, and a handful of fellow climbers knew where I was.

Friendships like these are crucial if you desire to stay engaged and motivated for years. Perhaps you can plug away for weeks or even months on your own, but I can't envision pouring yourself into anything year after year without life-giving community. We need each other.

The New Testament writings are laced with reminders about caring for each other. Here are a handful of the admonitions given to followers of the Christ:

"Love each other." (John 15:17)
"Serve one another." (Gal. 5:13)
"Carry each other's burdens." (Gal. 6:2)
"Encourage one another." (1 Thess. 4:18)
"Build each other up." (1 Thess. 5:11)
"Spur one another on toward love and good deeds." (Heb. 10:24)
"Confess your sins to each other." (James 5:16)
"Pray for each other." (James 5:16)

The clear evidence of Scripture is that we are not to navigate life alone. We were made for fellowship with God that bleeds over into our fellowship with each other.

So again, ask yourself, "Am I hiking alone? And does anyone know where I am?" I challenge you to invest in a circle of friends, long before you desperately need them. Cultivate relationships before the bottom drops out. We need each other. Create space in your schedule and in your heart for a group of fellow travelers. There will come a day when one of you needs help getting out of the canyon. We weren't meant to hike alone.

REFLECTION

Who are some travelers you can count on to hike with you and make sure you aren't going it alone? At the conclusion of the last chapter, you were asked to write down some of their names. Today, consider one or two of those names and reflect on when and where you can meet for fellowship, encouragement, and accountability. These relationships take time to cultivate. Begin to build into a couple of these people this week.

DAY 18:

SAMUEL'S CIRCUIT

CHRIS AND I RECENTLY RETURNED FROM VACATION—
a February escape that took us south for a brief retreat from the
frigid chill of Michigan winter. We enjoyed walking along the
beach, biking together, and boating with friends. As our plane's
wheels touched down back home, we were greeted by ten inches
of fresh snow. And then . . . back to work. Back to the grind.

I didn't return home to only a down jacket and a snow shovel.
I returned to a staff meeting today, a board meeting tomorrow,
watching our grandson on Friday, and preparation for our three
services Saturday and Sunday. Back to the people—and the string
of responsibilities—that mark so much of our lives.

In such moments, I need to remember that the daily grind we
return to is a life-giving grind. There's a word that describes the
consistency of showing up and serving people again and again.
It's the word *faithfulness*, and we hope that our lives are marked
by this quality.

It's healthy to periodically break out of the cadence of our
daily grind and visit new places, experience new activities, and

meet new people. However, much of faithful living is anchored in routine. Faithful, effective service to others often involves bringing ourselves to the same people, and often in the same way. Yes, this can feel redundant and repetitive, but it is largely where lasting influence lies. If you desire to live greatly, it will require a routine of offering faithful acts of service again and again.

Consider the great Old Testament prophet Samuel. The Bible highlights a handful of powerful, explosive events in his life. In one famous story, as a child being raised by Eli the priest, he is awakened in the night by the voice of God and utters the sentence that shapes his life and ministry: "Speak, LORD, for your servant is listening" (1 Sam. 3:9).

But then Samuel disappears from the narrative for several chapters. When the trusted leader surfaces again, he is a fully mature man, using his strong, prophetic voice to call his people to repentance (1 Sam. 7). In this crucial episode Samuel sparks a national revival.

As we turn the page to the next chapter, we anticipate yet another epic mountaintop event, but we are stunned to discover that Samuel is suddenly old. "When Samuel grew old, he appointed his sons as Israel's leaders" (1 Sam. 8:1).

Hold on! What happened? How could our hero be entering his senior years? Where did his life go?

The short answer is *the circuit*. Two uneventful verses summarize decades of faithful ministry: "Samuel continued as Israel's leader all the days of his life. From year to year *he went on a circuit* from Bethel to Gilgal to Mizpah, judging Israel in all those places" (1 Sam. 7:15–16, emphasis mine).

No spectacular military victory, no lightning from the heavens, no explosive event. Just a repeated circuit of faithfulness.

Year after year Samuel travels this judicial circuit from Bethel to Gilgal to Mizpah. In each location he provides counsel, gives spiritual direction, and offers judgment in challenging court cases. Again and again. Round and round. Over and over. I suspect this is what occupies Samuel's life when he is thirty-six years old. Fast forward the tape several years, and watch him at age forty-three, traveling the same familiar roads. What's he up to at age fifty-four? Ditto. Doing pretty much the same ministry with mostly the same people, in the very same places—Bethel, Gilgal, and Mizpah.

These verses are the sort that are easily skipped and often ignored. Nothing much happens, so we fly past them searching for the real action. Samuel moves from town to town in his annual circuit, administering justice and guidance to a generation of Israel's people—a picture of devotion, consistency, and faithfulness. And I'm certain the circuit also provided its share of monotony and tedium. Perhaps even boredom.

But Samuel's repeated ministry served to stabilize the nation at a time of desperate upheaval. When Samuel died, the people grieved. "Now Samuel died, and all Israel assembled and mourned for him; and they buried him at his home in Ramah" (1 Sam. 25:1). He was a steady, faithful, consistent source of guidance to his people. He was dearly loved and deeply missed.

LIFE ON REPEAT

Like Samuel's, your greatest impact in life could flow from repetition. If you succeed in serving, loving, leading, and blessing others, it will likely result from behaviors you have reenacted dozens—maybe hundreds—of times.

Whether you serve as a family doctor, a long-tenured volleyball coach, a parent of small children, or a camp director, I'm certain you have performed important tasks with dizzying repetition.

In my thirty-plus years of leading Ada Bible Church, much has changed. Responsibilities have shifted drastically since the days when our church family was composed of a couple dozen parishioners. But certain habits remain the same week after week, year after year.

I sit for hours each week and study, faithfully listening for a word from God—something to share with my congregation. On weekends, I stand on a platform and open the Scriptures to those who gather to listen, learn, and grow. This routine is basically the same today as it was three decades ago. Over and over, round and round, redundant and routine—and life-giving.

Each morning, I awaken, make coffee, and invite God into my day. I open my journal and pen a list of items for which I am grateful. I ask my Lord to flood my life with mercy, wisdom, and insight as I begin my work. I've done this literally thousands of times. And next week I will do it again. It's part of my circuit.

I remind myself from time to time that the price tag for transformation is redundancy. My diligent repetition brings life to someone else. If everything has to be new and interesting all the time, I will miss out on my greatest opportunity for impact and influence.

KEEP SHOWING UP

We need to be like Samuel. Find our circuit. Instead of view-ing redundancy as something to escape, we should see it as a life-giving force. We should show up and bring our best again and again.

Know this: It might not always be easy. Maintaining a consistent circuit isn't always comfortable or convenient. It usually involves bringing ourselves to many of the same people, in very similar ways, over an extended period of time. We are infatuated by overnight success and long for a quick fix. But this is not how an effective life is forged. It takes time to build anything of lasting impact. It takes real work. At the foundation of any outstanding, long-lasting influence is the challenge of showing up and putting in the effort—again and again and again. That's the heart of the faithful circuit—of dreaming big and thinking small.

REFLECTION

What is your circuit? Can you identify two or three tasks that you endlessly repeat in the service of others? Write them down here and realize how important and life-giving the daily grind actually is.

* _____

* _____

* _____

DAY 19:

DINNER. BATH. BED.

AS WE CONTINUE OUR CONVERSATION ABOUT LIFE-giving relationships, let's shift our attention to our families.

While much of this chapter revolves around our children, I realize your particular challenge may involve providing care for aging parents, helping with grandchildren, connecting with nieces or nephews, or building a healthy marriage. So today I want to extend the image of Samuel's circuit to family life. Often our greatest relational impact will come through giving ourselves again and again—especially to our family members.

GUYS' NIGHT OUT

A recent particularly memorable "guys' night out" for me was not a play-off game with a bunch of dudes in a friend's man cave, but instead an evening spent with my son and grandson. My wife and daughter-in-law were away at an event, so Alex and I decided to hang out at his place. While Alex made pasta, I played with Preston, who was eleven months old at the time.

Seated at their dining room table, I enjoyed Spaghetti Carbonara while shoveling vegetable puree into Preston. My pace of feeding him was unsatisfactory for the little guy, and the meal deteriorated as he smeared the luscious substance around his face and into his hair. I don't know when you last watched a baby feed him- or herself, but it's quite entertaining. It was truly a full-body experience.

With dinner complete, I extracted Preston from his high chair and shuttled him at arm's length to the bathtub for a much-needed ritual of cleansing. Then came the wrestling match to zip him into his footed pajamas before putting him to bed.

His parents have reenacted this sequence scores of times—this nightly rhythm of dinner, bath, and bed.

It might be monotonous sometimes, but stable families have a consistent, dependable rhythm. Around the edges, a creative family will embrace new activities and experiences. But look closely, and you will discover structured routine in their days, a dependable pattern built on redundancy and rhythm. Life and love are transmitted in these endlessly repeated activities.

Our three children came in rapid succession, arriving within a four-year span. How many diapers did we change? How many loads of laundry did we do? How many bowls of macaroni and cheese did we serve? How many bedtime stories did we read? Life on repeat.

I don't consider myself a model for balancing ministry and family. When I advise young parents who are trying to stay connected as a family while they're finishing a degree, building a company, or beginning a ministry, I have more to share from my failures than from my successes. But I do think I got a few things right.

TATTERED BOOKS AND GETTING IT RIGHT

A strip of duct tape graces the spine of our family's copy of *The Cat in the Hat*. The ragged condition of the cover bears testimony to the countless evenings our children selected this rhythmic volume for bedtime reading. I was elated when our eldest, Sarah, finally graduated from Dr. Seuss and we began to devour chapter books.

First we journeyed through the Chronicles of Narnia by C. S. Lewis. Later, as Andrew and Alex reached their grade-school years, I returned to these Narnia adventures of talking horses, young princes, mighty ships, formidable castles, and intense battles.

These well-used books still live on my shelf, and I grow nostalgic when the tattered, dog-eared set catches my eye. The three who curled up with me on the couch are now in their twenties, married, and two of them are parents themselves. The worn volumes remind me of hours we spent reading together. "This," I say to myself, "is something I got right."

I'm certain I'm not alone when confessing that my memories of enjoying my children are shadowed by the regret that I missed out on a lot. I regret being preoccupied on those evenings when I was physically at the dinner table but my mind was miles away. I regret those irretrievable moments when I was there, but not really there.

I'm so pleased that we wrestled, built campfires, and enjoyed picnics at area parks. But I fear I was emotionally absent too much of the time. Now that my children are grown, I wish for the impossible—that I could roll back the clock and have a "do over."

But during the evenings we spent reading, I was fully present—caught up in the same drama, sucked in by the unfolding storyline. And reading brought physical proximity, a rare commodity as the kids grew. Ask a second-grade boy to sit beside you for forty-five minutes without moving, and you have invited torture. But open to chapter thirteen, where Shasta rides into battle against the Calormenes, and you have guaranteed, uninterrupted snuggle time. Side by side, engrossed in the adventure.

Having shredded the Chronicles of Narnia, we worked our way through many of the Newbery award books. We read *The Slave Dancer, Rifles for Watie, Out of the Dust,* and *Number the Stars.* These stories opened windows of discovery to historic periods of the slave trade, the American Civil War, the Dust Bowl, and the Jewish Holocaust.

This is something I think I got right. But it was amid a myriad of moments that I missed. As we achieve and accomplish, plan and pursue, it's possible to miss out on the joy right in front of us.

DON'T MISS THIS

A young mother ventures forth on a grocery shopping expedition with two small children. Today her nine-month-old baby and toddling three-year-old are not cooperative shopping companions.

Then an older woman spies the frazzled trio and moves in on them. She smiles warmly at the exhausted mom, saying, "You're going to miss this." The weary mother nods respectfully, but thinks, "Are you crazy?"

Why does the older woman predict that these days will be missed? I think there may be a couple of reasons. First, she's probably forgotten the hard parts—the runny noses, the terrible twos, the middle-of-the-night diaper changes. This is important to mention because we tend to romanticize the past. Clearly, some elements of parenting are exhausting, frustrating, and mind-mushing. Things we have no interest in repeating.

But I think there is a second reason for the older advisor's comment. She misses parenting small children and knows she will never have it back.

I know it sounds cliché, but they grow up faster than you can possibly imagine. They begin so small. Tiny hands. Tiny feet. You bring them home from the hospital, and when you place them in your lap, they easily nest between your waist and knees. Unbelievably small. And then you turn around a couple of times, and they're enrolled in kindergarten. How did this happen? You look the other way, and suddenly they're in middle school, then driving, then wearing a cap and gown, and then grown and gone. You wonder where the time went.

When speaking to young dads, I frequently pose a math problem: "If your child were to move out of your home at age eighteen, at what age will you have spent half the amount of time that you will spend with them?"

I usually have to repeat the question, because the answer seems so obvious. After a second, the dad says, "Age nine. It's halfway to eighteen."

Ah, yes, but the actual amount of time they spend in your company diminishes as they reach middle school. As they begin to hang out with friends, participate in sports or youth group, or go away to camp for a week over the summer, their time in your presence begins to plummet. It evaporates further when they enter high school. And when they begin to drive, your home turns into a bed-and-breakfast.

So the real answer? I'm guessing that many of us reach the halfway point—in actual hours—when our child is about age six. So a word to those of you with young children: Don't miss this. In your preoccupation with making partner or building a church or completing your dissertation or keeping a household running, don't miss this. They will never be this size again, and you will never have this much time with them again.

Now, perhaps you have young children, but reading to them is not what will draw you together. Maybe it's biking or hiking or music or cooking. But find something! Discover a common enjoyment and repeat it over and over and over. Time moves at dizzying speed. Turn your head and they are grown and gone.

Don't miss this.

YOUR CURRENT INVESTMENT

Again, your current challenge may not be raising children. This chapter might enter your life as you drive weekly to a nursing home to visit a parent, or as you prepare for premarital counseling, or as you care for a granddaughter two days a week. But we're still drilling down on the same principle. Much of faithful living involves bringing ourselves to non-spectacular tasks again and again. It's the power of showing up. Of listening. Of hearing. Of loving consistently.

Act swiftly. Time flies. Opportunity evaporates. Make sure you don't miss this. Take the time to do the little things—day after day, week after week, year after year.

REFLECTION

What family member might be particularly in need of your attention or love in this season of your life? Narrow your focus so you can take specific, immediate action with one individual. Do you have a lonely parent who is hinting at a need for your company? Is this perhaps the season to step up your time with a grandchild to grant a bit of margin for your own kids? Is one of your children struggling a bit right now and could really benefit from some extra attention?

Take a moment to identify one name.

_____

Now reflect on a way to engage this person. Think of an activity, event, or new routine you can do together to build that connection.

_____

_____

_____

_____

DAY 20:

HOW WE HEAL

IN OUR CONVERSATION ABOUT LIFE-GIVING RELATION-
ships, it's important to recognize that friendships can be some
of our greatest source of pain and confusion. As you love and
serve people faithfully over an extended period of time, you
may face the real temptation to throw in the towel because of
repeated injury.

In Week Five we will be talking about major mistakes that
threaten to derail us. That will be a crucial conversation, because
there are legions of men and women whose lives and impact are
compromised by a moral failure or an ethical train wreck from
which they never fully recover. But here, as we close out Week
Four, I want to recognize another way to finish badly. It's not a
single regrettable mistake that brings our world crashing down
around us, but a slow and steady injury of the spirit. We quit
because we're tired of getting hurt. We walk away not because of
a massive, disqualifying mistake but because of the accumulated
effect of unhealed wounds.

Let's begin this conversation with a reality check. If you love and serve people well, you will get hurt. In *The Four Loves*, C. S. Lewis wrote:

> To love at all is to be vulnerable. Love anything and your heart will be wrung and possibly broken. If you want to make sure of keeping it intact you must give it to no one, not even an animal. Wrap it carefully round with hobbies and little luxuries; avoid all entanglements. Lock it up safe in the casket or coffin of your selfishness.[1]

To love is to put your heart at risk. Relational pain is inevitable and unavoidable for those who open their hearts to others. This reality helps us understand another major barrier to finishing the race.

REALITY BITES

Many of us begin our work or ministry life with youthful idealism—not a utopian dream, mind you, but an expectation that people will behave themselves. Then reality bites, and we turn skeptical of people and organizations. Uncorrected, our skepticism flows downhill, creating a deep, black pool of cynicism. This dark swamp is a wretched foundation for loving, serving, and leading others.

So how do we heal from this? Can we recover in a way that leaves us softhearted and approachable? Resilient? Or are we hardening ourselves, refusing to let anyone get close enough to hurt us? Healing well is crucial to finishing well.

THE SONG OF BETRAYAL

In Psalm 55, King David of Jerusalem penned a tortured lament. His sad song tells not only the story of wounded betrayal, but also of extraordinary guidance on healing the wounded heart.

Listen first to his tale of pain:

> *If an enemy were insulting me,*
> *   I could endure it;*
> *if a foe were rising against me,*
> *   I could hide.*
> *But it is you, a man like myself,*
> *   my companion, my close friend,*
> *with whom I once enjoyed sweet fellowship*
> *   at the house of God,*
> *as we walked about*
> *   among the worshipers. (Ps. 55:12–14)*

David is hurting. He's been wounded by a colleague. Not an enemy, not a foe, but a dear friend. The sort of friend with whom he once shared a strong spiritual bond. David's wound is one of life's most painful—the discovery that someone you trust has turned on you.

No life is without pain. Throw yourself into loving and serving, and it's only a matter of time before you are lacerated by hurtful barbs said to you or about you, or saddened by the departure of a beloved colleague with whom you envisioned a much longer run. Petty complaints take their toll. The whisper of a gossip bruises your reputation. You get roughed up in a meeting or suffer when your most ardent supporter becomes your most vocal critic.

Unattended, our wounds fester. Left alone, they get infected. *We* get infected. Perhaps we continue to lead, but we become like cast iron, shielding ourselves from the possibility of future hurt. We grow unapproachable, distant. Embittered.

How do you heal from that kind of pain? Where can the heart turn when you feel deceived and disillusioned?

Gordon MacDonald wisely confesses, "We have to admit that, in the process of leadership, there are moments of extreme disappointment and disillusionment when people we lead utterly fail to live up to our expectations."[2]

MacDonald asserts that it is wise to ask how leaders of the past "resolved their anger, discouragement, and blaming spirit that threatened to overwhelm their souls."[3]

So in this overwhelming challenge, where did King David take his pain? How did he resolve his anger, the discouragement, and the blame?

TENACIOUS TRUST

Let's return to David's song, where tenacious trust rises from the melody:

> *As for me, I call to God,*
> *and the LORD saves me.*
> *Evening, morning and noon*
> *I cry out in distress,*
> *and he hears my voice. (Ps. 55:16–17)*

The betrayed king calls out to God. Knowing that the pain and confusion are way beyond his own capacity to heal, he invites his God into the mess. He pleads for the Lord's help in this overwhelming disappointment. He runs to him for rescue.

But don't assume this is a quick or easy process. David cries out to God "evening, morning and noon." This wasn't the kind of wound healed by a single prayer. In his confused sadness, David calls out to God in the late hours of the day, as the sun rises in the morning, and in the routine of his midday responsibilities. I get the feeling this was the last thing he thought about when he crashed at night and the first thought that entered his mind as his feet hit the floor in the morning.

The king's song drips both pain and confidence. The Lord, he says, "hears my voice."

David throws his anxiety on his Lord. His gracious God hears. The Creator sustains him to lead and serve yet another day.

LIFE-GIVING COUNSEL

The wise king now turns his attention to the listener. Up to this point, the psalm has chronicled David's pain and healing. Now he gets prescriptive. He offers counsel to the wounded and betrayed. "Cast your cares on the LORD and he will sustain you" (Ps. 55:22).

How to heal effectively? The answer is undoubtedly multi-faceted. Healing can involve the grace of trusted friends and perhaps the guidance of a counselor. But don't miss the obvious. Cast your cares on the Lord. A faithful, enduring life requires a continued dialogue with our Lord, who guides, loves, and heals.

So where do you turn when you're hurt, bruised, beaten up? Where do you look when abandoning the race is an enticing alternative to the possibility of incurring future pain?

I don't want this to sound trite or sappy, but our odds of staying in the race climb dramatically when we engage in brutally honest conversations with God about how things are going. We vent, weep, and maybe rant about what's happening—and how we *feel* about what's happening.

Listen again to God's wounded but healing servant:

> *As for me, I call to God, . . .*
> *Evening, morning and noon*
> *I cry out . . .*
> *and he hears my voice.*

He listens. He sustains. He gives the strength to go another mile.

He gives us the mercy to stay in the race.

REFLECTION

What might you need healing from? A person who hurt you?
Dreams that have gone unrealized? Skepticism or negativity that
has crept into your life? Write it down here.

_____

_____

_____

_____

Where can you turn for healing? How does God promise to
bring you through this season of life?

_____

_____

_____

_____

WEEK FIVE:

STRESS FRACTURES

ACCIDENTS AND INJURIES

Each July the world's best cyclists compete in the Tour De France, arguably the most grueling endurance race on the planet. The route covers over two thousand miles in twenty-one stages over twenty-three days. The cyclists are pushed to the limit over exhausting mountain passes and punishing time trials.

On the official Tour De France website you can view the leaders for each stage. You can also see a list of those who have withdrawn from the race. In three weeks of taxing competition, injury and accident take their toll. Not everyone who starts the race will finish.

You may not be a world-class cyclist, but if you pursue a life of faithfulness, you will find yourself in a challenging endurance race. It's sobering to remember that not everyone will reach the finish line.

In Week Five we'll explore some of the most common accidents and injuries that force good people out of the race.

DAY 21:

THE FINISH LINE

IN GRAND RAPIDS, MICHIGAN, EACH YEAR, THOUSANDS of runners compete in the 15.5-mile (25K) River Bank Run. The field boasts world-class athletes, but many of the runners simply compete against the mileage, desiring to mark a fitness achievement both challenging and rewarding.

Because the race is held in early May, training begins in the heart of Michigan's winter. Trust me, it's not particularly pleasant weather to be running in. Consequently, the fulfillment in crossing the finish line is not only completing the race, but also celebrating the successful accomplishment of months of bone-chilling preparation.

Hundreds of participants begin their running careers only months before the race. They summon the motivation to endure a winter training regimen, gradually building their fitness base, increasing their mileage week by week. Then on race day, many run farther than they have ever run in one stretch in their lives.

The route carries you away from the city, west along the Grand River, before you make the turn to head back toward town. The distant skyline seems impossibly far away. In the final half mile you ascend Ottawa Avenue, and the finish line comes into view. You summon whatever remaining strength you possess and push the final hundred yards. As you cross the finish line, a volunteer greets you with a finisher's medal.

I have completed the River Bank Run about twenty times and have discovered a comic sentimental attachment to my finisher's medal. Immediately, it becomes a prized possession—more treasured than my car, my college diploma, my house, or my firstborn child. I exaggerate slightly, but you get the point. I ran into an acquaintance whose wife wore her medal around all day. A friend in his mid-twenties slept in his.

Now, I need to repeat that this is a *finisher's* medal. It's not a trophy for coming in first, second, or third. It's not even an award reserved for those who place well in their age group. Everyone who finishes this race gets one of these treasured medallions, which they hand out by the thousands. It doesn't matter that three thousand other people own an identical medal. You did this! You finished this race!

FINISHING WELL

The term "finishing well" feels threadbare from overuse. When powerful imagery becomes cliché, we grow immune to its force. But I find that this race image captures my deep longing to love and serve for a very long time without my spirit being poisoned by resentment, apathy, or cynicism. I also aspire to end my run, however long it may be, without adding some massive train wreck to my résumé.

I long to finish well, and I am acutely aware that not everybody does achieve that. I'm a bit surprised that, after years of faithful ministry, the apostle Paul still considered disqualification a possibility. To a Jesus community in southern Greece he wrote, "I do not run like someone running aimlessly; I do not fight like a boxer beating the air. No, I strike a blow to my body and make it my slave so that after I have preached to others, *I myself will not be disqualified for the prize*" (1 Cor. 9:26–27, emphasis mine).

Paul embraced rigorous spiritual training—I run . . . I box . . . I strike a blow to my body—to ensure that he would not get DQ'd. He didn't want to be stripped of his medal. He wanted to complete his race.

On another occasion Paul borrowed Olympic imagery as he tearfully said farewell to church leaders from Ephesus. Certain that he would never see his beloved friends again, he was also convinced that he would face severe hardship and imprisonment in his near future. Things looked bleak for the seasoned servant. For what did Paul long at this stage of ministry? To finish the race! "I consider my life worth nothing to me; *my only aim is to finish the race* and complete the task the Lord Jesus has given me—the task of testifying to the good news of God's grace" (Acts 20:24, emphasis mine).

Standing on the eastern shore of the Aegean Sea, the apostle Paul said good-bye to his dear friends from Ephesus. His desire? "I just want to finish the race!" He had a job to complete, mileage yet to run. He summarized his particular race as "the task of testifying to the good news of God's grace."

Grace is that aspect of God's character that is wildly generous. He gives and gives and gives. Paul looked ahead to a distant finish line. His goal was to use every ounce of energy, every breath, to tell others of the generosity of God in sending Jesus for us.

Let's face it, many of the races we enter are decidedly less noble. We race to buy more of what we already have too much of, or we run after approval, or we compete for popularity. Paul's race? He desperately wanted people to comprehend the generosity of God that is discovered in Jesus the Christ. That was Paul's event, and he longed for his finisher's medal.

Toward the end of his life, Paul wrote from a Roman prison to his colleague Timothy. He believed his time on earth was short. Listen to the runner:

> *I have fought the good fight,* I have finished the race, *I have kept the faith. Now there is in store for me the crown of righteousness, which the Lord, the righteous Judge, will award to me on that day—and not only to me, but also to all who have longed for his appearing. (2 Tim. 4:7–8, emphasis mine)*

Paul looked up to see the last yards of his race, the finish line, and the medal that awaited him there. With deep satisfaction he announced, "I have finished the race!"

ARE YOU STILL IN THE RACE?

The next chapters are possibly the most sobering of the book because they deal with the secret lives we lead, the threat of moral failure, and the diligence required to stay the course. Please bring a soft, humble heart to these chapters.

From the bottom of my heart, I long for you to complete the

race God has called you to run. A finisher's medal awaits you. I long for you to finish well.

REFLECTION

Are you still in the race? How are you dealing with the disappointments that have inevitably come your way? Are your wounds festering or healing? Are you caring for your own soul so you can care for the souls of others? Are you tempted to walk off the track? Will you finish well? Write down some of your thoughts here.

_____

_____

_____

_____

_____

As we prepare to begin this next week together, please read the following prayer out loud:

Gracious Lord, I confess my daily need for your strength and your grace in my life. I am lost without your daily provision and protection. Please give me a humble and teachable spirit this week. Soften my heart to hear your clear voice. I long to finish well. Amen.

DAY 22:

THE FOUNDATION

A WALK IN THE WOODS

Brittle leaves crunch beneath our feet as the six of us hike the three-mile trail not far from my home. The temperature spikes into the low seventies, uncharacteristically warm for a late October day in Michigan. I run here regularly and know the route well, but the path is new to everyone else. My five hiking companions are younger pastors. We meet every few months, often in a coffee shop, but today I want to focus our conversation from a specific place we will pass on our hike.

About thirty minutes into our walk, we pause at the site where a barn once stood. The structure is long gone, and today only the foundation is visible. Mature trees rise around the space that once housed livestock and farm implements.

I've halted our hike at this location to reflect on that part of our lives nobody sees—the foundation, the world that lies beneath the surface. That space where holy disciplines and hidden sins grow. It is from this interior, private world that our public lives will thrive or falter. For better or worse, who we are in private usually manifests itself in public.

I've selected this site and bring up this sobering topic because of a growing casualty list.

- The computer system of a hookup website is hacked, exposing the double lives of public figures.
- A professional athlete is besieged by the media when allegations of domestic violence surface.
- The sketchy financial practices of a politician threaten to ruin her career.
- A pastor is forced to resign after repeated complaints that coworkers and board members fell victim to his controlling, demeaning rage.

Above the ground all seemed well—a thriving career, a growing ministry, a satisfied constituency. But trouble brewed beneath the surface. And major regions of neglect threatened the whole structure.

You might be a highly gifted, unbelievably talented man or woman who genuinely affects hundreds of lives with impact. But if and when an implosion occurs, it will be difficult for those exposed to the rubble to remember your positive, life-giving side. When secret habits—those concealed below the surface—are exposed, it will be challenging for others to remember the positive aspects of your character and ministry. It might not be fair, but we are more remembered for a devastating fall than for steady goodness. When a house burns to the ground, the foundation is all that is left to see.

Oswald Chambers used the imagery of "who we are in the

dark" to urge his readers to pay attention to what was happening beneath the surface of their public lives:

> We are only what we are in the dark; all the rest is reputation.
> What God looks at is what we are in the dark—
> The imaginations of our minds;
> the thoughts of our heart;
> the habits of our bodies;
> these are the things that mark us in God's sight.[1]

And so the six of us pause beside the aged foundation of the barn and talk about our public worlds and our private worlds. About what is above the surface and what lies below the surface. I take the conversation very seriously, believing the stakes to be immeasurably high. The private habits of these five men greatly affect the health and vitality of five congregations. And apart from the impact on their churches, the hidden lives of these men will affect their five families; together, they have over a dozen children. I am hopeful that our conversation will fend off some future tragedy, that we might detect patterns of sin and weed them out while they are still small and operable.

As we stand at the site of the old barn, we speak openly of our own struggles and challenges. We share of ongoing temptation and success and failure. We talk about our foundations, the part nobody sees. Or rather, that nobody sees for the time being but someday may be exposed to in a manner we cannot predict or control.

And so we hike, and pause, and talk. We talk about who we are when nobody's watching and the difference it makes. I wish everyone had a space for such honest dialogue.

WHAT'S BELOW THE SURFACE?

It's important to periodically ask ourselves what is brewing below the surface of our lives. That part of us nobody sees. Recall the passage from Proverbs we explored on Day 12: "Above all else, guard your heart, for everything you do flows from it" (Prov. 4:23).

What is the condition of your heart? Does any bitterness grow, threatening to poison your relationships? Do any wounds fester, unattended and unhealed? Does any lust rage? Are any hidden sins nursed, unobserved by all but God? What is growing below the surface?

This is also the space where we quiet ourselves before our Creator, where we plead for mercy, confessing that we are not right. Our hearts are the soil where grace grows, where healthy roots plunge deep, nurturing life above ground.

Rarely does anyone drive past a house and admire the foundation. But it is the foundation that supports the rest of the structure. An enduring public life is supported by a vigilant private life.

A PLEA

What did you find when you looked beneath the surface of your life? Did you acknowledge the presence of something that deeply troubles you—a poisonous attitude, a gaping wound, an embarrassing habit, or secret addiction? If you are reading this and believe you've really made a mess of things, please reach out to those who love you and can help walk you out of the darkness. Know that your first impulse will be to cover up your mess, to keep your problems hidden. The threat of exposure can be paralyzing.

Here we face a monstrous challenge. A destructive, hidden behavior drains our life away. But voluntarily exposing our darkness to someone feels suicidal. It might be long and hard and complicated and painful, but I plead with you to deal with what grows in your private world. I plead with you to seek the wisdom of a skilled friend or pastor or counselor who can speak God's mercy and direction into your life. It is highly unlikely that you will find your way out of this on your own.

Trust that there is someone out there who can enter the tangled mess and walk with you toward holiness and healing. Trust that God is not done with your story. Trust that lasting, life-giving transformation is often found on the other side of an embarrassing revelation. Trust that God's redeeming grace desires to bring you home and that he will show convincing evidence of his mercy along the path.

Believe that there is hope. Remember that many who finish well suffered an ominous setback in the middle miles. It's not too late to get back in the race. It's never too late to begin building on a new foundation.

REFLECTION

Reflect upon your foundation. What do you see when you look beneath the surface of your life? If you see a tangled mess— something you can't solve by yourself—you need someone you can turn to for help. Write down the names of several people you can count on when your foundation begins to crack or crumble.

_____

_____

_____

DAY 23:

THE FALL

AT THE CONCLUSION OF A CHAPEL SERVICE AT OUR small Bible college, six of us were called to the office of the Dean of Students. We were from the same northern California community, and our immediate fear was that there had been an accident and we were being gathered to receive the tragic news collectively.

Instead, the dean informed us that a beloved pastor from our area had fallen morally. The news stunned and saddened us; his messages at various camps and retreats had made a significant impact on all of us. He'd been a guiding voice in our adolescent years. This was not some distant personality but a leader we loved. We knew his kids. We hurt for his family and his church. The affair ended his marriage and, to my knowledge, he never returned to ministry.

This is my first recollection of learning that someone I trusted had lost his way morally.

You and I are naïve to believe we are immune to moral failure, to think ourselves somehow incapable of devastating those we love and serve. A fall can happen to any of us.

There are, of course, other ways to capsize a life:

- A college senior is expelled for fabricating data in a research project.
- A salesperson is canned for misusing her expense account.
- A coach resigns when his explosive tirades are caught on film.
- A night of overindulging results in a suspended driver's license, a huge fine, and the possibility of jail time.

I think you get the picture. We can derail our effectiveness and damage our impact in a variety of creative ways. But in our conversation on finishing well, I need to dial in on one particular threat. Specifically, I want to press a conversation about why moral failure is so common and what you can do to lower the odds of appearing on this growing casualty list. Of all the ways to implode our lives and destroy our reputations, moral failure seems to be topping the charts. It feels epidemic.

Why does this seem to happen with such regularity? Let's break it down by analyzing the anatomy of an affair.

ANATOMY OF AN AFFAIR

They've worked in the same office complex for over two years, barely noticing each other. But in the recent corporate restructuring, their departments merged. Marketing and sales now share the same floor, the same break room, and the same support staff. As they begin to interact with each other, the term "mutual admiration" best describes their relationship. She's smart, competent, and funny. He's articulate, caring, and witty. They admire each other. That's all.

As they begin to collaborate on projects, he asks about her life—her interests, hobbies, and background. He's genuinely interested and listens attentively. This gift of focused attention is something she feels her husband rarely provides. In her twelve-year-old marriage, she feels undervalued and underappreciated. She also feels unheard.

But at work she feels as though someone has opened a window. Fresh oxygen fills the room. Her new colleague offers heartfelt thanks for her attention to detail and her ability to creatively view a challenge. Through simply offering encouragement and appreciation, he's feeding her longing to feel noticed and enjoyed. Without making a conscious decision, she begins to select her work outfits with greater care.

And let's explore his life for a moment. The other end of his commute is far less affirming than what he experiences from his new, energetic coworker.

His marriage isn't awful, just plagued with the chronic challenges of any enduring relationship. Awaiting him at home is a conversation about an overdue credit card bill and a question about when he intends to fix the dripping faucet. The evening exchange concludes with an exasperating realization that a parent/teacher conference conflicts with his sales meeting.

And he's tired. Meetings, decisions, and appointments have drained him. He feels little energy and motivation to provide what he has given at the office—focused attention, affirmation, and eye contact. And, truth be told, he longs to feel valued.

At the office the next day, the two people in question pour

their energy into a joint presentation. Though their work is labor intensive, they feel refueled and refreshed. They laugh. The pitch is for a potential client in another city. They look forward to a break from the office, the opportunity to bring new business to their company, and time with each other. They will fly together, stay in the same hotel, and enjoy a well-deserved glass of wine at the end of a long day.

BLINDNESS

Now, if anyone from the office suggested that something illicit might be brewing, they would deny it vehemently. Why? Because *they* don't believe anything is going on. They don't see that they are both emotionally famished and depending on each other for emotional fuel.

As they make final tweaks to the presentation and pack their carry-on luggage, they are oblivious to the reality that the emotional entanglement they're getting sucked into could result in the implosion of two families.

Affirmation intoxicates, impairing our judgment. We begin a tragic slide, feeling we are being pulled toward something healthy, filling, life-giving. The heart is capable of massive self-deception.

THE WANDERING HEART

Most affairs don't begin with meeting in a hotel room. They usually begin in far more subtle, innocent ways.

If you are starved for emotional connection, if you are lonely and tired, affirmation from someone you find even mildly attractive can be drug-like. We crave more of it and begin to organize our schedules and traffic patterns around being in proximity to the person who makes us feel valued and valuable. Consciously—or subconsciously—we begin to order our weeks around getting our next fix.

And a side note especially to those of you in ministry. . . . If you entered ministry out of a longing to be needed (which is exceedingly common), and if you want to have an impact on people through authentic heart connection (which is what much of ministry is), and if you have difficulty connecting deeply with your spouse and friends (which is also common), then you are already set up for a fall.

Sober vigilance is required to keep on track. There is no sure formula for affair-proofing your life, but in the next chapter, I will offer some practices that may increase your odds of finishing well.

As I reflect back on the meeting in the dean's office my freshman year in Bible college, I know I desperately want to avoid a day when those I've loved and served are gathered to hear such an announcement made about me. How can you guard *your* heart so that such a revelation is never made about you, whatever your job or calling? I long for you to avoid such a day, with its heartache, betrayal, and fallout. Please read the next chapter with focus and prayer. The advice, if heeded, could rescue you from a lot of pain.

REFLECTION

As you think about your life right now, where are you in possible danger? Reflect on how your thirst for affirmation could lead to devastating decisions. Do you have any seemingly "innocent" relationship that could bring heartache to those you love? Here and now, ask God to remove any blindness and to give you the courage and strength to back away from a relationship that could capsize your life.

_____

_____

_____

_____

_____

_____

_____

DAY 24:

AVOIDING A FALL

I HAVE OBSERVED MANY WHO FINISH THE RACE DESPITE a massive fall. A huge mistake doesn't count you out from finishing well. There is a redemptive storyline that reads, "I fell flat on my face, destroyed my reputation, devastated my family, but then I got back up, experienced God's grace and healing, and now I'm moving forward again."

This is a beautiful redemption narrative. It speaks to God's mercy and his heart to restore. But it's also a narrative I hope you get to avoid, a narrative that involves gaping wounds and horrendous scars. Personally, I'd rather have my story read, "I sought God's grace daily and, by his mercy, somehow avoided a major mess."

SMART STUFF

There's no sure formula for affair-proofing your life. However, I do believe a number of practices will dramatically increase your odds of avoiding moral wreckage.

• Be Aware

Know yourself. Foster a healthy belief in your own depravity—your ability to fall. Don't be naïve! Repeat after me:

> "I am not immune. I am capable of an infinite amount of self-deception. I have the capacity to wreck my life in creative and unimaginable ways."

• Build Healthy Friendships

We increase our chances of moral failure when we endure prolonged stretches of loneliness. Often we are lured into a destructive relationship because we have not expended the time, energy, and focus to invest in constructive relationships. Build real, healthy relationships—with your spouse, your kids, your buddies. It is your responsibility to cultivate healthy friendships. (It might be rewarding to reflect back to Days 16 and 17 and revisit the importance of building life-giving relationships.)

• Don't Run on Empty

Beware of a perpetually empty gas tank. If we continuously pour ourselves out without replenishing our depleted souls, there will come a day when we demand, "I'm taking care of everybody! Whose gonna take care of me?" and a tender, sympathetic voice whispers back, "I will."

Running on empty sets you up for disaster. There is a point of exhaustion where we grow indifferent to the pain we are about to inflict. As we barrel down a road of indiscretion, if someone challenged, "Don't you realize who you are about to devastate? Don't you see how this decision will cripple your husband, your children, your church?" our fatigued voice could bark back, "I DON'T CARE!" Beware of reaching a point beyond caring.

• Establish Distance

Do you detect that someone other than your spouse (or, if you are single, someone who is married) is feeding you emotionally and you are lapping up the attention? Begin immediately to establish distance. This will probably feel wrong, because being near him or her is so filling. Resist the gravitational pull of their orbit. Don't hang out! Create space.

King Solomon pleaded with his listener to establish distance from a possible affair. Listen to part of his counsel from Proverbs 5:

> *Now then, my sons, listen to me;*
> *do not turn aside from what I say.*
> *Keep to a path far from her,*
> *do not go near the door of her house. (vv. 7–8)*

There, in that last line—"*do not go near* the door of her house." Keep yourself well away from those environments where you can easily find yourself enticed to do something ruinous.

• Don't Let On

This certain someone makes you feel important, humorous, or attractive. There is a possibility that you make them feel valued, interesting, or beautiful. Don't, and I mean NEVER, tell them how you feel.

Consider these innocent-sounding questions:

"Don't you feel like we have something special?"

Or,

"Do you ever wonder if we had met before we married other people if we would have gotten together?"

These are probes. They are adult versions of the sixth-grade note:

> *I like you. Do you like me?*
> *Check Yes, No, or Maybe.*

If someone interests you, do not hint in any way that anything could happen between you. No possible good can come from this.

COSTLY MERCY

If you have failed morally, this need not be the end of your story. By God's mercy, many get back in the race following a disastrous fall. God is telling redemption stories at every turn.

King David slept with the married woman next door and then schemed to have her husband killed in battle to cover up the resulting pregnancy. When confronted by the prophet Nathan, he repented, owning the crimes he had committed. Psalms 32 and 51 are songs written in this season and reveal David's broken, humbled heart before God and his longing for forgiveness and spiritual cleansing:

> *Then I acknowledged my sin to you*
> *and did not cover up my iniquity.*
> *I said, "I will confess*
> *• my transgressions to the LORD."*
> *And you forgave*
> *the guilt of my sin. (Ps. 32:5)*

This is a beautiful song of grace and restoration following a moral failure. But I hope you are able to avoid singing these lyrics altogether. These expressions of mercy come at the high cost of immense damage to ourselves and to others.

Some finish well but cause massive pain along the way. Do everything you possibly can to avoid this storyline. But if you have fallen badly along the course, know that God can pick you up, dust you off, and run with you all the way to the finish line. His grace makes it possible. Get back in the race.

REFLECTION

What are some things you can do to be aware of potential stumbling blocks in your own race? What are some healthy friendships in which you can invest? How can you keep your tank full so you aren't running on empty? How can you establish distance when you need to? Write down some action steps here:

_____

_____

_____

_____

_____

_____

_____

_____

DAY 25:

WHO ARE YOU FIGHTING FOR?

OUR LIVES CHANGED IN MARCH 2014 WHEN CHRIS AND I became grandparents. Before Preston's birth, I didn't fully calculate the extent to which this critter would capture our hearts. Two years after Preston's arrival, we were greeted by Cooper and Hazel. We are truly smitten, and we look forward to every opportunity to be with our children's children.

Part of the allure of grandparenting is that you experience the intense joy without all the sleep deprivation. I'd heard the well-worn punch line dozens of times: "And then you get to give them back." But the cliché is true. We hang out with our grandchildren in manageable doses, and then return them, freed from the perpetual demands of parenting.

But this new era of life has given me even more reason to think about finishing well. I'll be in my sixties when these darlings are in grade school. And what kind of sixty-year-old will they encounter? Will they find me generous and kind, or will I be an embittered old soul—grumpy and impatient? Will my countenance invite or repel? Will Grandpa be a joy or a misery? What kind of old guy am I becoming?

I've been given yet another reason to finish strong. A toxic heart drives our loved ones away, while a healthy spirit invites others to draw near. I'm not fighting only for me; I'm fighting for those I love.

REBUILDING THE WALLS

When I reflect on those who depend on my faithfulness, I'm drawn to a speech given by the biblical character Nehemiah. In 586 BC, Jerusalem was totally destroyed by the Babylonian army. Generations passed and the city remained in ruins. After a century, Nehemiah worked to restore the honor, dignity, and safety of the city by rebuilding the defensive walls that circled Jerusalem.

In Nehemiah 4, the walls reach half their intended height, but the workers are exhausted and feel incapable of summoning the strength to complete this monumental task. At this crucial moment, the residents of Jerusalem learn that regional warlords are preparing to attack their city. As the crisis unfolds, we see Nehemiah at his finest hour. Here is his own account of his response: "I stationed some of the people behind the lowest points of the wall at the exposed places, posting them by families, with their swords, spears and bows" (Neh. 4:13).

This is a desperate situation. Nehemiah assigns workers to guard the most vulnerable places along the wall, equipping them with swords, spears, and bows. These weapons are useful at varying distances. A bow can repel an enemy fifty yards away. But a sword? If you have to use your sword, the conflict is right on top of you. A sword is up close and personal. You can see your enemy's eyes, almost smell his breath. And by the way, those reconstructing the wall—and now guarding it—aren't professional soldiers. They are goldsmiths, perfume makers, farmers, shepherds, and the like. These people are scared!

How will Nehemiah bolster their courage?

Notice that he positions the defenders "by family." Why did he do that? He arranged them so they were fighting alongside their cousins, uncles, brothers, fathers, and sons. If attacked, they would be fighting not only beside their families, but *for* their families. Listen to Nehemiah's speech: "Don't be afraid of them. Remember the Lord, who is great and awesome, and fight for your families, your sons and your daughters, your wives and your homes" (Neh. 4:14).

I find it compelling that, while challenging them to defend their sons, daughters, and wives, Nehemiah doesn't tell them to defend themselves. I can defend myself if I run away and hide, but I can't defend *anyone else* if I run away and hide.

I find Nehemiah's challenge highly motivating. We can be at our most cowardly and self-centered when fighting for nothing more than ourselves. And we are at our most courageous when we are fighting for someone else.

In his book *Deep Survival*, Laurence Gonzales recounts chilling stories of life and death struggles from desperate survivors adrift at sea to bewildered hikers lost in the wilderness. He shares his understanding about who lives, who dies, and why:

> Helping someone else is the best way to ensure your own survival. It takes you out of yourself. It helps you to rise above your fears. Now you're a rescuer, not a victim.[1]

This is a profound insight. Often we pull ourselves together in a desperate situation because others are depending on us.

WHO ARE YOU FIGHTING FOR?

Who are you fighting for? This is a crucial question for those of us who long to finish the race well. After all, if no one is counting on you, go ahead and throw in the towel. Why go to all the work of cultivating an enduring spirit or generous heart if no one is depending on you? *Who are you fighting for?*

This is why I contemplate what kind of "old guy" I will become. . . . I desire to age with grace because of the rings of people whose journey I influence. The inner ring includes my wife and children (and now the grandchildren who have been added to that ring). The next ring is composed of close friends and work colleagues. Another sphere encompasses the congregation I am privileged to serve. I continue outward to yet another, unseen ring—those who may enter my life a decade from now.

This last ring deserves special mention. We should guard our hearts on behalf of those we have yet to meet, who are not currently in our lives but will be someday. I mention this, believing that the habits of today affect the relationships of tomorrow even if those relationships are currently unknown and unnamed.

I frequently encourage unattached men and women to work toward financial stability before they get engaged—to bring financial discipline to their future marriages. I encourage husbands and wives to work on their anger issues before children enter their home. The added strain of parenting won't make emotional self-control easier. The time to cultivate a heart for ministry is years before entering ministry.

I am becoming the person I will be. Decisions of my heart today forge the man I will become tomorrow. My effectiveness, love, and service years from now will grow from the seeds I plant today.

But this only functions as a motivation if I am fighting for someone other than myself.

So who are you fighting for? Who depends on your courage and perseverance? Whose life is bolstered by yours?

This is why you should long to finish well. It's not just about you. Your life is woven together with the lives of others. Even those you have yet to meet. So don't just fight for yourself. Also fight for those whose lives are enriched by yours.

REFLECTION

Create a list of those whose lives are influenced by your faithful stability. List the names of those whose lives are impacted by yours. List immediate family members, people in your friend group, individuals you serve and lead. In addition to listing those in your inner ring, list those in your second and third ring of influence.

Inner Ring: Immediate Family

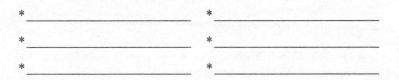

Second Ring: Close Friends

*_____   *_____

*_____   *_____

Third Ring: Those You Serve or Lead

*_____   *_____

*_____   *_____

Read these names out loud, slowly envisioning each person.

WEEK SIX:

REVISITING SUCCESS

THE DIRECTIONS ON MY PACKET OF INSTANT OATMEAL read:

> Empty packet into bowl
> Add ½ cup of boiling water
> Stir

That's it. Oatmeal. Instantly—or nearly so.

I love the promise of immediacy, but I fear we have fostered a culture of impatience. We desire instant everything. I'm not thinking here primarily of oatmeal, but of instant results. Instant impact. Holiness grown in a weekend.

But a life that truly shapes and deeply blesses others is long in the making. There is nothing instant about it, and those afflicted by impatience will definitely miss out.

So here in Week Six—our last week together—let's turn our hearts once again to the long, faithful road to greatness.

DAY 26:

THE TABITHA FACTOR

THE BIG MOVE

It's the first morning of the conference. You've checked in, received your name tag, and selected a seat in the balcony. Following the opening video and welcome, the first speaker is introduced. You open your notebook to a fresh page and write the speaker's name in the upper left-hand corner. You intend to take notes.

The story that pours from the stage is riveting. The speaker and her husband were dutifully following the American Dream script—college, career, cars, house, lawn, furniture, cottage, retirement, and then death. But then they sensed a powerful stirring that capsized their comfortable lives. They began to desire more.

Her words resonate with many of us:

"We wanted our lives to count."
"I didn't want to reach the end of my one and only life

to discover it had been wasted on things that didn't really matter."

"We believe God created us to make a difference."

Then came what she calls the Big Move. They sold their house, gave their furniture away, got rid of their cars, and reduced their personal belongings to the contents of four large duffel bags. They moved to a needy Central American country where they opened a youth center to serve disadvantaged teenagers.

Today, eighteen years later, they genuinely thank God for the lives that were transformed through their work. Among the graduates of their program are three doctors, thirteen nurses, eight schoolteachers, a dozen pastors, and a Bible college president.

Her final sentences are well-crafted and delivered with conviction:

> "These lives were transformed forever because of the move we made eighteen years ago."
>
> "There is a better script for your life than the American Dream."
>
> "Move when God tells you to move."
>
> "Go where he calls you to go."
>
> "Be willing to make the Big Move."

She folds her notes and steps off the stage. The room erupts in heartfelt applause. You look at your notebook and see an empty page where you had intended to take notes. As the session concludes you scribble your summary:

I want my life to count. Go where God tells me to go. Make the Big Move.

LOOK AGAIN

I don't want to spoil the impact of talks like these, and I don't want to diminish the work God inspired in that ministry, but I need to point out something.

The lives of those teenagers were not changed because the speaker and her husband sold everything and moved to Central America. Those lives were transformed because, once they arrived in Central America, *each and every day* this faithful woman and her faithful husband awakened, left their apartment, caught a bus, and opened the doors of their youth center, where they poured themselves into the slow, painstaking work of discipleship.

Talks like these tend to emphasize *the move* while giving brief mention to the challenges of many years of devoted ministry. Make no mistake about it—the Big Move this couple made *was* risky and heroic. It was an obedient response to God's unique call upon their lives. The move was the catalytic event that set things in motion, but these lives were positively affected because of the slow, persistent work that occurred *after* the move.

This is a significant distinction. Though possibly set in motion by a jarring event, your greatest impact will still need to rest upon steady, disciplined servanthood. It's what I call the Tabitha factor.

THE TABITHA FACTOR

Tabitha is dead, and a Christian community mourns. The grief-stricken believers summon the apostle Peter, who can hear the weeping before he even reaches the front door. Widows are crying, mourning a loss too heavy for them to bear. Acts 9 recounts the gripping story:

> *In Joppa there was a disciple named Tabitha (in Greek her name is Dorcas); she was always doing good and helping the poor. About that time she became sick and died, and her body was washed and placed in an upstairs room. Lydda was near Joppa; so when the disciples heard that Peter was in Lydda, they sent two men to him and urged him, "Please come at once!" (Acts 9:36–38)*

When Peter arrives, he is taken to the upstairs room where Tabitha's body lies. A group of widows surrounds him, weeping and showing him the robes and other clothing Tabitha made for them.

Desperate poverty was the common experience of widows in Eastern culture. In the world of the Bible, life could be unbearably difficult for a woman who had lost her husband and had no adult sons or brothers to care for her. Tabitha stepped into their distress and devoted her days to reducing the suffering of those who felt very much alone.

Knowing this, imagine the tear-streaked faces of the widows who now surround Peter. Hands lift garments and grief-filled voices repeat, "She made this for *me*."

What did a new cloak or robe mean to these widows? The clothes Tabitha made for these destitute women meant warmth, dignity, and hope.

Joppa, where the story occurs, was on Israel's Mediterranean coast. A cloak protected against the cold winter winds that whipped off the sea. Tabitha's goodness provided shelter from the cold.

But apart from the functional aspect of clothing is the element of dignity. Did a widow feel more dignified after exchanging a threadbare robe for one that was new and beautiful? Tabitha's goodness diminished shame and enhanced self-respect.

I believe the clothing Tabitha wove with her own hands also brought these women a strong dose of hope. When a widow received a new garment from Tabitha, a voice whispered, "Someone's looking out for you. You are not alone."

Warmth, dignity, and hope. Tabitha is a hero of the early church, and her death was a tragic loss. But now step back for a moment and examine what Tabitha actually did. I mean functionally, what occupied her days? The text doesn't say she *purchased* clothing for these widows but that she *made* the clothes.

Please grasp this. Tabitha lived an extraordinary existence by devoting herself to fairly unextraordinary activity. When you break it down, what Tabitha did wasn't all that sensational. She spent day after day sewing. Tabitha's legacy was that she engaged in the time-consuming process of making clothing by hand and then giving these items away to those who were financially desperate. This feels a bit . . . well . . . boring to me.

Day in and day out, Tabitha sits and sews. If you were to view her through a window, at any given moment her task would look simple, ordinary, and perhaps tedious. What was spectacular about Tabitha was the sheer consistency and faithfulness of her devoted love. She did this again and again and again.

HOLY REPETITION

Most of us desire to live great lives. We fear we will fritter away our days without leaving any discernible mark on our world. But in our quest to live greatly, we search for something great to do. Something BIG. I believe this to be a huge mistake.

Greatness is rarely achieved by doing great things but instead by doing good things repetitively. The tragedy is that, while waiting for *great* opportunities to come along, we miss out on a parade of *good* opportunities that march steadily by. Goodness is largely ignored because it seems too common, too mundane, too everyday. Tabitha arrived at greatness through a lengthy corridor of goodness. That's the Tabitha factor.

Tabitha was a rare and remarkable woman because she embraced a holy redundancy, day in and day out. Above her life hangs a motto that reads, "And then she got up and did it again."

While "random acts of kindness" may benefit people's lives for a moment, the ministry of Tabitha seems significantly different. Her devotion to the widows of Joppa doesn't feel "random." Nor do we sense we're viewing a series of isolated "acts." There is a difference between an act of kindness and a lifestyle of goodness, and Tabitha discovered the latter.

Through her compassion, Tabitha provided an astounding model of consistent service, performed in love, for those who needed it most. It's a beautiful legacy to follow. This seamstress is a hero of the early church.

BACK TO THE CONFERENCE

The first conference session comes to a close and the applause dies out. You have just heard the remarkable story of a couple who awakened day after day for eighteen years and sought God's grace, mercy, and wisdom as they served vulnerable teenagers.

Yes, the Big Move launched their impact, but that wasn't what defined it. Their influence was defined by a daily faithfulness. A holy redundancy that announced, "Today we will do it again."

REFLECTION

Before you close out this chapter, reflect on your own life.

Identify one consistent "Tabitha task" you are willing to give yourself to repeatedly.

_____

_____

Think of three people in your world who faithfully reflect the Tabitha factor—perhaps a parent or coach, a volunteer at your church, or a servant in your community.

* _____

* _____

* _____

Take time today to reach out to one of them and thank them for their faithfulness.

DAY 27:

WHEN NOBODY'S WATCHING

OLYMPIC SPEED SKATING CHAMPION APOLO OHNO appeared in a television commercial extolling the nutritional value of chocolate milk.

In the ad, Ohno races up a flight of outdoor steps in a strenuous workout. He leaps from side to side as he ascends the long staircase. The grueling drill continues as, feet together, he jumps up the stairs, clearing three steps at a time.

The music intensifies as the Olympian voices, "Momentum. The power to keep pushing. The discomfort zone." The first time I saw the commercial, I was struck by a single compelling sentence that eclipsed the hype and promotion of the advertisement. The eight-time Olympic medalist recalled the counsel of his father: "My dad used to say, 'Champions are made when no one is watching.'"

Ohno is referring to the countless hours spent in the gym and weight room and on the practice skating track. To the years of dedication and perspiration—largely unobserved and unap-plauded. The payoff occurs in a packed Olympic stadium, but the foundation is forged through thousands of training sessions in relative solitude. No cheering fans. No thunderous applause. No TV cameras. Champions are made when no one is watching.

I suspect most meaningful pursuits require a similar sort of training, a space where public effectiveness is built through private discipline. When you enjoy the performance of a gifted pianist or cellist, be assured that the inspiring music is a result of years of practice. The stirring platform presentation is backed by thousands of hours of solitary rehearsing where no one was watching. When observing a moving concert, I muse, "I wish I could play like that." But while I wish I could play like that, I have no interest in practicing like that. Yet one is necessary for the other to become possible.

DAILY DISCIPLINE

Indulge me for a moment as I draw upon an example from my profession. While you may never find yourself in a situation where you are asked to deliver a sermon, I trust that this example will apply to your field.

From time to time I'm asked to speak to seminary students on the topic of preaching. For more than three decades, I've worked to develop the art of effective communication and covet opportunities to dialogue about the subject. So occasionally I find myself in front of a classroom, attempting to inspire men and women who are delivering their first sermons or may have a teaching role in their near future.

Frequently, I've asked students to name their favorite preachers. Who do they download religiously? Who inspires and challenges them? Who would they wish to emulate? The students respond, naming well-known speakers with whom they resonate.

I then encourage them with, "If you desire to teach with that level of effectiveness, don't attempt to copy what they are doing while *on* the platform. Instead, discover what they're doing when they are *not* on the platform. Imitate that instead."

A good question is, "How do they present?" A better question is, "How do they prepare?" Discern what study habits and daily disciplines make compelling communication possible, I tell the students. Inevitably, those who are effective in ministry over the long haul have embraced private practices that undergird public ministry. To revise Apolo Ohno's line, effective communicators are made when no one is listening.

Public performance is one thing. Private discipline is another.

Transformational sermons are birthed in solitude, requiring extended time glued to a chair. When effective sermons are finally delivered, they may be deeply engaging, powerfully illustrated, and life-changing. But they aren't all that interesting to write. They result from a redundant process that looks pretty much the same week after week.

First come hours spent reading and re-reading a passage of Scripture, scouring the pages of commentaries for borrowed insight, note-taking, and drafting a structured outline. We offer humble prayers, asking our Lord to whisper what he longs for his people to hear. Then comes crafting illustrations, crossing the cultural bridge from the world of the Bible to our generation with the intent of bringing hope, comfort, and conviction to the people sitting in front of us.

While much of my study time is spent developing the sermon I will deliver that weekend, a large segment is reserved for cultivating ideas that will not reach the platform for months. This advance preparation allows a passage of Scripture or a biblical character to grow on my heart, germinating over time. This is not as easy as it sounds. The pressure of immediate and urgent situations conspires to drive out planning for the future. Don't underestimate the discipline required to focus forward as present crises plead for your attention.

The end result of consistent, disciplined study time may be a compelling sermon that God uses to transform people's lives, but the work to get to that point is rather uneventful. A guy sits in a chair for hours with a Bible, laptop computer, and commentaries. Again and again and again. For years. If there is an honest shortcut to the process, I haven't discovered it yet.

By the way, if you didn't find the last few paragraphs very interesting . . . well . . . that's the point. So much of the life-giving work we diligently repeat isn't glamorous.

NO APPLAUSE

Perhaps you hold no aspirations to compete in the Olympics or perform beautiful music or deliver effective sermons. But excellence in any meaningful area of life requires steady, faithful discipline.

Apolo Ohno represented America in the 2002, 2006, and 2010 Winter Olympics. In these competitions, he took home two gold, two silver, and four bronze medals. The Olympics are highly public events, but these medals were earned in private.

Your most important moments may be those nobody sees and nobody applauds.

REFLECTION

Reflect upon and answer this question: "What single, quiet activity could make the biggest difference in my personal, professional, or spiritual life?"

_____

_____

It's probable that the activity you wrote down could go largely unobserved and generally unapplauded. But remember, champions are made when no one is watching.

DAY 28:

THE BIG EVENT

AT THE BEGINNING OF WEEK SIX WE TALKED ABOUT THE Big Move and why transformational growth usually occurs because of the devoted work that happens *after* the move. The same holds true for the Big Event. It's important for us to explore the incredible opportunity as well as the limited capacity for major events to transform our lives.

THE RETREAT

I recovered my faith in the Sierra Nevada Mountains of northern California. I was fifteen years old, and turbulence had marked the preceding three years of my life. Seventh grade was marred by the sudden death of my mom in an automobile accident. Eighth grade brought a challenging move from Idaho to Michigan, along with my father's subsequent remarriage. My freshman year of high school was a time of settling in, before the announcement of yet another cross-county move—this time from Michigan to

California. My sophomore year began in a new state, a new school, and a new church. Spiritually, I was adrift.

As a recent arrival, I accompanied my new youth group on a camping trip to Lake Tahoe where, seated in an amphitheater under the stars, I listened to a sermon on the obscure biblical character Balaam. The speaker concluded by asking us if it was time to restore our hearts to God. I knew he was speaking to me. I have no memory of the contents of the sermon, but I count the message as one of the most important in my life. That night served as a catalyst for the spiritual movement that followed through the remainder of high school.

The camping trip that turned my heart required a ton of preparation. I was oblivious to the organizational intricacies at the time, but I am now aware that you don't haul sixty teenagers into the mountains without first reserving campsites, securing tents, making careful preparation for meals, arranging transportation, and recruiting a speaker who can deliver a killer sermon on Balaam.

Events like this require hundreds of hours of planning, are often expensive to host, and generally exhaust those responsible for their execution. Whether you find yourself organizing or merely attending a major event, I think it is important to have a candid conversation about their value and limitations.

The types of events I have in mind here include:

- Taking a week off work to participate in a short-term mission trip.
- Canceling plans for a weekend to attend a marriage conference.
- Sitting in a large auditorium, soaking in the words of a motivational speaker.

Let's talk about what these major events *might* accomplish, what they usually *don't* accomplish, and the *emotional hangover* that is the common aftermath for those on the organizational side of these undertakings.

WHAT THE BIG EVENT MIGHT DO

The Big Event frequently serves as a catalyst for significant movement. This is what I experienced in the Sierra Nevadas my sophomore year of high school. A funeral, a wedding, and two cross-country moves had been highly disruptive for me. I was at a crucial crossroad, and the retreat propelled a new direction in my life.

This is why we organize events like this, and this is also why we attend them. These experiences draw us away from our ordinary routines, providing a fresh opportunity to hear the voice of God. Many of us came to faith at camp, reevaluated our dreams while on a mission trip, or reengaged in church following an elaborate Easter production. Big events can be extremely valuable because our Lord often uses them to launch new movement in our lives.

WHAT THE BIG EVENT DOESN'T DO

While functioning as a launchpad for needed movement, there is something the Big Event doesn't do. It doesn't grow us up. Unfortunately, we don't mature in a weekend, and there is a difference between a catalyst for growth and growth itself. When the Big Event results in significant change, it is generally because of what we do *following* the event, not what happened *during* the event.

Thousands gather in an arena to be inspired by a nationally known financial guru. He's insightful, entertaining, and motivational. But those who experience lasting change in their spending and saving habits are those who actually *do* something when they get home. Specifically, our odds of building an emergency fund and getting out of debt rocket if we join a step-by-step budgeting class *following* the arena event. Then there are those thorny little details like actually implementing the budget. Big Events get us moving, but it's impossible to escape the necessity of long-term follow-through.

Or consider the standard summer camp experience. Scores of teens make decisions during a week at camp, but good intentions evaporate at an alarming rate when kids pile into vans and wave good-bye to their counselors, the serenity of the lake, and the flames of the campfire. I suspect the teenagers who experience the greatest lasting change are those who get connected to positive influences upon their return home. This was my experience following the campout in the Sierra Nevadas. Following the retreat, I came under the daily influence of a dynamic soccer coach as well as a phenomenal youth pastor. The retreat served as a spark to get the fire going, but the fire had to be refueled—again and again—to stay alive.

There's no replacement for steady growth over a sustained period of time.

Remember this the next time you carve out precious time to attend a weekend conference or retreat. The nature of a two-day event is that you arrive in need of a refreshing drink of water and depart feeling like you've attempted to drink from a fire hose. It's natural to walk away with your head spinning from a hundred great ideas. A good practice is to ask yourself, "Out of everything I've heard over the last couple of days, what are two things that—if implemented faithfully—could make a massive difference in my personal, vocational, or ministry life?" Faithful implementation of two new practices will far outdistance non-implementation of a few dozen grand ideas.

For those of you who organize and orchestrate big events, remember that lasting change from your labor will likely result *following* the completion of these events. This can be disheartening, because successful completion of a major event feels like we've crossed a finish line. We pull off the conference, retreat, concert, or trip and announce, "Done!" But from a standpoint of real growth, the event serves more as a starting line than a finish line. We now embrace the rather routine, daily, mundane grind of follow-through.

And that leads to a new challenge. The hangover.

THE HANGOVER

Let's face it. Hosting big events can be exhausting. So tiring, in fact, that little energy remains for the routine that must follow for lasting impact. Let me offer a word of advice to those of you who pour yourselves into these exhausting endeavors.

Consider the church worship team that envisions the Easter service to end all Easter services. They hold countless planning sessions, conduct a string of late-night rehearsals, and double the number of services on Easter weekend. They encourage church members to invite friends and family who have strayed away from church over the years. The weekend arrives and all the planning pays off. The services are outstanding and are sure to make an impact. A triumph. You trust that hundreds of guests will return to the church the following weekend.

Oh . . . yes . . . the following weekend. Sundays seem to roll around with amazing regularity. A weary haze hangs over the Tuesday planning meeting. The team looks hungover. They sleepwalk through their planning session, summoning what little reserves they have left. The tank from which they draw creative energy has run dry. They jettison recommended creative elements because there is no energy left to pull them off. After charging into Easter weekend, they now drag into their weekly routine.

What will returning guests experience the following Sunday? Will they feel like they have walked through the doors of an entirely different church?

For those of you who organize major gatherings, the challenge is to expend enough energy to create a profound experience while also reserving enough resources to sustain the routine work that must follow. Imagine a gas gauge, like the one on the dashboard of your car. How will the fuel tank read when the Big Event is over? Be cautious of draining the tank dry. The opportunity for real, lasting impact begins when the big event ends. So make sure you have something left in the tank!

REPEAT AFTER ME

Those of you who attend or organize major events, please repeat after me:

- It is highly unlikely that total transformation will occur in a weekend.
- It is certain that the most profound growth will be a by-product of work we do *after* the Big Event.

Go ahead and enjoy the momentum generated by an enthusiastic crowd or on an exciting trip. Capitalize on the surge of motivation you receive from an outstanding weekend of fresh information. These experiences can be crucial to our growth. But it always comes back to steady movement in a life-giving direction, undertaken one day at a time. Whether you are navigating life as a family, starting a company, or rebuilding your life piece by piece, it pays to dream big, but think small.

REFLECTION

Think of the last Big Event you attended. What were your hopes going into the event? Did the event propel you to head in a new direction, or were you too overwhelmed to make changes or implement any steps for action? What is one small thing you can do today—and tomorrow and the next day and the next—to effect lasting change in your life?

_____

_____

_____

_____

_____

DAY 29:

THE WALL AND THE WEEDS

CHRIS AND I LOVE WALKING THE HISTORIC STREETS OF Grand Rapids. Many of the hundred-year-old homes are well maintained, a tribute to the time and perspiration that have lovingly been poured into these valued properties. Other houses, however, are dwellings that have been neglected and poorly maintained. They are run down. Paint peels. Overgrown shrubbery obscures the view from the front window. Our eyes glance upward to loose shingles, and we imagine the water damage on the interior of these homes.

Realize that you don't have to do anything for a property to fall into disrepair. All you have to do is leave it alone. The seasons take their toll. Sufficient neglect guarantees deterioration of a house and a life.

THE VINEYARD

King Solomon meditated on this reality while taking a walk. In Proverbs 24, the wise monarch records his reflection as he passes a neglected vineyard. The protective wall is crumbling. Weeds overtake the ground, choking the life from fruit-bearing vines. He observes this badly maintained field and draws some stunning conclusions about the impending financial disaster that awaits the owner.

Listen to Solomon's observations about the wall and the weeds:

> *I went past the field of a sluggard,*
> *past the vineyard of someone who has no sense;*
> *thorns had come up everywhere,*
> *the ground was covered with weeds,*
> *and the stone wall was in ruins. (Prov. 24:30–31)*

The vineyard, with such promise of fruitfulness, has fallen into disrepair. The abundance of weeds and thorns provides ample evidence that the owner of the property lacks the energy to maintain this valuable asset. The wall, painstakingly constructed years before to keep predators out, has deteriorated.

The culprit? Simple, sustained neglect.

I imagine the owner protesting, "Why are you criticizing me? I didn't do anything!"

Yeah. We can see that. For a vineyard to deteriorate, all you have to do is *nothing*.

ENTROPY

The guy in Solomon's passage didn't go into his vineyard and knock the wall down. He didn't have to. It simply crumbled to ruin over time.

If you want weeds to take over a garden, leave it alone. They are adept at finding their way in all by themselves. You don't have to plant them. You don't have to cultivate them or fertilize them. Weeds just happen.

Weeds can also grow in our lives. Envy. Bitterness. Slow-burning rage. We can awaken to discover their presence and demand, "Where did *you* come from?"

The sobering reality is that we don't have to do much of anything for our world to cave in. There is a subtle inertia in the most crucial areas of our lives. Things don't get better on their own, but they do tend to decline on their own.

All you have to do to become an embittered old person is nothing. Just allow the wounds of life to take their natural course, sending roots deep into your soul. You awaken one day to discover that your heart has been taken over—slowly, gradually—by the poisonous vines of a bitter spirit.

If you take your eyes off the road, the car is bound to end up in a ditch sooner or later.

- The gradual effects of careless spending result in sudden financial meltdown.
- An unmaintained heart allows petty resentments to accumulate, building and growing until cynicism dominates our spirit.
- Our most important relationships collapse under the accumulated weight of unresolved conflict and uncorrected drift.
- Marriages end after suffering slow erosion over the course of many years.

Things unravel by doing nothing. Weeds grow. Walls crumble. Lives implode. Slow and steady faithfulness will result in a harvest. So will slow and steady neglect.

SLOW EROSION AND SUDDEN DESTRUCTION

King Solomon reflected long and hard on the weed-infested vineyard. He observed the broken-down wall and the thorn-covered estate and drew a profound conclusion:

> *I applied my heart to what I observed*
> *and learned a lesson from what I saw:*
> *A little sleep, a little slumber,*
> *a little folding of the hands to rest—*
> *and poverty will come on you like a thief*
> *and scarcity like an armed man. (Prov. 24:32–34)*

A little sleep, a little slumber. We view a man devoted to harmless lazing. Carefree and unworried, he naps. As he snores, the wall goes unrestored. Stones dislodge and topple. A minor incident, really—a rock here, a rock there—uneventful and unnoticed. As the man sways in his hammock, weeds grow. Day after day, inch by inch, thorns creep in relentless invasion of the precious soil, choking out the valuable vines. A little sleep. A little slumber.

Did you notice the contrast between the slow, drowsy pace of the owner's slumber and the sudden implosion of his world? Observe the change of pace: "Poverty will come on you like a thief and scarcity like an armed man." Someday this guy will awaken and feel like he's been mugged.

All of a sudden, so it seems, things fall apart. But the "sudden" disaster has been long in the making. While neglect occurs gradually, the collapse usually feels sudden.

"*All of a sudden*, she moved out and got an apartment."

"*Before I knew it*, we received a foreclosure notice."

"*Suddenly*, I discovered I didn't have a friend in the world."

While it is possible for us to destroy our lives through a single, enormous blunder, what King Solomon describes here is a more subtle path to ruin. The mess is achieved through apathy. Not a single huge mistake, but slow and steady neglect. It's like Ant Power in reverse.

I want to pause for a moment and give a word of encouragement to those of you who are suffering the "sudden" effects of prolonged neglect. Often our gracious Lord is pleased to use a financial, emotional, or marital earthquake as a wake-up call. Don't let your pain be wasted. Use this challenging, humbling experience to begin building your life in a new and different way. The pathway to a renewed life often passes through seasons of disorienting failure. Don't lose hope. Today is a new day.

WEEDING AND REPAIRING

How, then, do we prevent the crumbling of our lives? How do we restore the vineyard after seasons of neglect? We've got to get our hands dirty. We must devote ourselves to perpetual weeding.

A flourishing vineyard demands continual care so that the weeds don't steal the nutrients needed by the vines or consume the water needed by the grapes.

It's important that we begin the weeding process in our lives today, that we refuse to let gradual neglect lead to catastrophe.

I know this effort can seem daunting. So I encourage you to choose one weed to pull at a time. Think small. Don't go after every weed at once, but pick one you can pull out of your life in the next twenty-four hours. Life will not be mended in a day, but you can start somewhere and begin to restore the vineyard to its full glory.

REFLECTION

Can you detect some weeds that you need to pull from the soil of your own life?

- What grudge are you nursing?
- What thorny habit threatens to take over the soil of your soul if you continue to let it grow?
- What cancerous attitude could cripple your spirit if you allow it to thrive?
- What key relationship is slipping away one day at a time?

Take a moment to reflect on your life. Write a couple of sentences recognizing a weeding project that comes to your mind.

_____

_____

_____

_____

_____

_____

DAY 30:

GOODNESS GROWS SLOWLY

THROUGHOUT THIS BOOK I HAVE CHALLENGED YOU TO Think Small—to devote yourself to repeated positive activity that grows steadily over time.

The challenge with this type of movement is that you rarely detect forward progress from day to day. The same cannot be said of tragedy, which crashes into our lives with deafening force, upending us in moments. Coming to grips with the slow speed at which goodness travels is critical if you are to maintain the long, persistent journey of faithfulness.

EVIL STICKS

One beautiful May evening, my friend Dale and I strolled through the Colonial district of Santo Domingo, Dominican Republic. The next morning we were scheduled to visit a children's hospital run by CURE International, an outstanding ministry that provides critical surgeries in under-resourced countries around the world. They also excel at sharing the story of Christ with families who bring in their children for medical care. In short, their mission is to heal kids and tell people about Jesus. Many of the regions served by CURE are marked by volatility and violence.

As we walked in the warm Dominican air, we talked about the tragedy that had occurred one month earlier when a gunman opened fire at the CURE hospital in Kabul, Afghanistan, killing three American doctors. As our conversation unfolded, we had an unforgettable dialogue about the nature of good and evil. "Evil sticks," Dale mused, "but goodness has a really short shelf life."

When evil is enacted, it has staying power. Evil doesn't need to be reaffirmed. But to leave a lasting imprint on people's lives, goodness has to be reaffirmed time and time again, continually, over a lengthy period of time.

Over its first dozen years, the CURE hospital in Kabul had served more than 700,000 outpatients and performed 21,000 surgeries. In a country that had been ranked as one of the worst places in the world in which to give birth, CURE workers have delivered more than 25,000 healthy babies.

"Three American Doctors Gunned Down in Afghanistan" is likely to gain CNN headline status. "Afghan Mother Gives Birth to Healthy Baby" is decidedly un-newsworthy. Evil grabs attention. It's simply more press-worthy than goodness, which grows quietly over time. Goodness doesn't make a lot of noise. It is a quiet virtue.

THE ACCIDENT AND THE COACH

Consider the way this plays out in a small community. A town mourns the accident that claimed the lives of three teenagers. Tragedy struck with screeching tires and twisting metal. The horrific news sweeps through the high school with the devastating shock of a tsunami. Bouquets and handwritten notes form a spontaneous memorial at the intersection where the cars collided.

Tragedy strikes.

Conversely, goodness rarely "strikes." It arrives on the stage with little drama.

In the same community that experienced the awful accident, a devoted coach painstakingly builds a cross-country program for middle school girls. For a dozen seasons, she forges diligence, teamwork, and confidence. Some of these girls are the products of affirming, encouraging homes. But others will remember their seventh-grade cross-country coach as "the first person who believed in me."

Twenty years pass. Ask a thirty-three-year-old woman from the community what influences impacted her while she was growing up. Reflecting for a moment, she answers, "The Accident" and "The Coach." But these arrived at different speeds and in radically different ways. Tragedy strikes. Goodness grows slowly.

As I reflect on my own life, I recognize the formative impact of both jarring tragedy and steady love. I awakened one November morning in my seventh-grade year to learn that my mom had been killed in an automobile accident during the night. The sudden loss of my mom is the most singularly defining event in my early life. But my life was also profoundly shaped by my mother's steady presence and deep affection. I remember her laughter, her gracious eyes, her presence when I raced home from the bus stop and barged into the house. From my earliest moments, I believed that I was securely loved.

DO NOT GROW WEARY

The snail's pace at which kindness travels will require extreme devotion to the journey. Goodness demands staying power. The question is whether we will summon the requisite endurance for a slow, faithful, consistent outpouring of love.

I believe this is why the apostle Paul urged an early community of Jesus's followers:

> *Let us not become weary in doing good,*
> *for at the proper time we will reap a harvest,*
> *if we do not give up. (Gal. 6:9)*

When Paul encourages, "Let us not become weary in doing good," I believe he is saying, "Don't get tired of doing this, because lasting impact will require that you devote yourself for a really long time."

Paul addresses the issue of weariness because a life of goodness can be tedious and redundant. It involves bringing ourselves again and again, often to the same tasks and often to the same people. The repetition takes something out of us. It drains our energy. Paul was writing here of the kind of weariness that leads to calling it quits.

Awaken one morning and breathe the prayer, "Lord, today I offer my life to You." The next morning, do it again. And again. And again. Eventually, is there not a real temptation of awakening one day and muttering, "This is getting really old. I just don't feel like doing this anymore"?

On such a morning, it is imperative to remember the law of the farm. Did you see the agricultural imagery Paul selected?

. . . we will reap a harvest, if we do not give up.

How I wish he had selected a different metaphor. Perhaps something with a little more speed, quicker results. But, no. Paul went with farming. You can't rush a harvest. You plow, you plant, and you wait. There's a gap between burying a tomato plant in the soil and enjoying salsa months later.

I believe the farming image can radically adjust our expectations. Sometimes a life of positive impact is about as interesting as watching a garden grow. Personally, I'd rather throw myself into a cause and see fruit after a couple of intense weekends. But I bet Paul was familiar with our craving for overnight success—our desire for immediate results. He went with a farming illustration. You plant. You wait. Goodness grows slowly.

So keep showing up. Keep planting. Do not grow weary in doing good. The harvest will come.

A DAY AT THE HOSPITAL

The day after our stroll and conversation about the shooting in Afghanistan, we visit CURE's Dominican hospital in the heart of

Santo Domingo. After a tour of the facility, we sit in a small room where the surgical director examines patients. Parents accompany their children who were operated on weeks or months earlier. The surgeon gently moves limbs to test range of motion, tenderly asking questions. Assessing progress.

I sit in the corner and observe the first examination. Then the second. Then the third. Routine. Nothing monumental. Nothing sensational or flashy or newsworthy. Just an ordinary, everyday, follow-up examination. And . . . I'm growing bored by the time we get to the fourth patient. I get the idea. I don't need to see a dozen exams to understand how the system works. An endless parade of opportunity. Conversation after conversation. Child after child. Showing up and doing pretty much the same thing again and again. Faithful ministry anchored in repetition.

This is what these wonderful people do to bring healing and demonstrate the compassion of Jesus. It's slow and steady. It's loving and beautiful. But it isn't headline-grabbing.

Goodness rarely crashes upon us with deafening impact. It arrives instead through the repeated kindness of the diligent faithful. It arrives quietly, traveling the slow path of devoted love.

I urge you to Dream Big but to Think Small. Day by day, one loving act of kindness after another, you have an opportunity to grow a life of greatness. Do not grow weary in doing good. The harvest awaits you.

REFLECTION

Before you close the book, I urge you to turn the page and explore the exercise in the conclusion. Tomorrow is an important day. What consistent practices will become part of your life? It's essential to think over what has stirred your heart and mind over the last six weeks and focus on two or three elements that will fuel your faithful life. Find some quiet space, turn the page, and reflect on your next steps.

CONCLUSION:

NARROW YOUR FOCUS AND BEGIN

OVER THE LAST SIX WEEKS WE'VE EXPLORED HOW LIFE'S greatest investments require steady, faithful movement over the course of time. This principle holds true as we raise a family, build a God-honoring career, cultivate a healthy heart, and develop strong friendships.

As we close out our time together, it is essential that you narrow your focus to two or three behaviors or disciplines you can immediately put into practice. Perhaps these are areas already in motion—priorities that seized you in earlier weeks. Consistent movement in two or three areas will carry you farther than twenty new ideas that quickly evaporate.

Let me encourage you to use a two-step process for narrowing your focus.

FIRST

Skim through the book to see what you marked, highlighted, or wrote in the Reflection segment at the end of each chapter.

When something jumps out at you as a strong potential priority or suggestion, write it down in one of the spaces below. Attempt to reduce your list of potential next steps to a maximum of ten options.

1. _____

2. _____

3. _____

4. _____

5. _____

6. _____

7. _____

8. _____

9. _____

10. _____

SECOND

Read your list slowly and thoughtfully. Ask God to lead you as you reflect on the ideas and priorities you just wrote down. Now, of those ten areas, which two or three should immediately begin to find space in your heart and calendar? It is important to be specific. Don't merely write down a name or a discipline, but take time to write out specifically how this repeatable priority will evidence itself each week. What exactly do you plan to do, and where will you carve out time to do it?

1. _____
   _____
   _____

2. _____
   _____
   _____

3. _____
   _____
   _____

Remember, you are unlikely to see immediate results. Goodness grows slowly. Your greatest movement will be measured over the course of months and years, not over the course of a few days.

I would like to close this book with my sincere prayer for all of you who are embarking on this adventure of dreaming big while thinking small.

May our gracious God deliver you from the illusion of overnight success.

May he provide daily strength, daily courage, and daily wisdom as you pursue the faithful life.

May your journey be filled with hope and joy.

May you experience the pleasure of God and hear those words we all long to hear: "Well done, good and faithful servant!"

ACKNOWLEDGMENTS

TO MY WIFE CHRIS, WITH WHOM I HAVE SHARED THE journey of life and ministry. Thanks, Babe, for your encouragement, love, and patience through another book project.

I am deeply grateful to the Zondervan team whose hard work and dedication made *Dream Big, Think Small* possible. Special thanks goes to Carolyn McCready. Carolyn, thanks for believing in this project from the beginning and guiding me through the writing process. I also want to thank Jim Ruark and Jean Bloom for their outstanding editorial assistance. Much appreciation to Alicia Kasen for her help and guidance along the way.

My appreciation to Wolgemuth and Associates—Erik, Andrew, and Robert—thanks huge. Erik, I am deeply indebted to you for our early conversations that helped form the focus and direction of this book.

Major thanks to Marsha Sweet, my gracious ministry assistant, who works tirelessly to help keep the various aspects of my ministry life together.

I am indebted to Susie Finkbeiner for reading through my initial draft of *Dream Big, Think Small* and offering helpful comments on how to improve the material.

Special thanks to a special group: Aaron and Afton, Rich

and Ash, Chris and Jess, Jesse and Kristi, and Chris and Hallie. Thanks for the evenings spent in our home reflecting on the material. Your comments were so valuable in shaping these pages.

Finally, I wish to express my appreciation to the congregation of Ada Bible Church. I am deeply grateful for your faithfulness week in and week out. Your open and receptive hearts make ministry a delight.

NOTES

Introduction

1. David McCullough, *The Wright Brothers*, reprint (New York: Simon and Schuster, 2015), 113.

Day 1: A New Kind of Hero

1. François Fenelon, *The Seeking Heart* (Auburn, ME: Christian Books, 1992), 133.
2. Ibid., 182.

Day 3: Mister Rogers

1. The information about Fred Rogers comes from various websites.

Day 4: The Mobile History Lesson

1. Jim Collins, *How the Mighty Fall: And Why Some Companies Never Give In* (New York: Collins Business Essentials, 2011), 92.

Day 5: The Twenty-Mile March

1. Jim Collins, *Great by Choice: Uncertainty, Chaos, and Luck—Why Some Thrive Despite Them All* (New York: HarperBusiness, 2011), 61.

Day 10: Recovery

1. Charles H. Spurgeon, *Lectures to My Students* (Peabody, MA: Hendrickson Publishers, 2010), 170.

Day 12: A Dialogue with Your Soul

1. Gordon MacDonald, *Building Below the Waterline: Shoring Up the Foundations of Leadership* (Peabody MA: Hendrickson Publishers, 2011), 40.

Day 14: Remembering Who You Are

1. Henri J. M. Nouwen, *Life of the Beloved: Spiritual Living in a Secular World* (Spring Valley, NY: Crossroad Publishing, 1991), 35.

Day 17: The Circle

1. Laurence Gonzalez, "One Way Out," *National Geographic Adventure* (August 2003).

Day 20: How We Heal

1. C. S. Lewis, *The Four Loves* (New York: Harcourt Brace, 1960), 147.
2. MacDonald, *Building Below the Waterline*, 132.
3. Ibid.

Day 22: The Foundation

1. Oswald Chambers, "The Ministry of the Unnoticed," *The Love of God: An Intimate Look at the Father-Heart of God* in The Complete Words of Oswald Chambers (Grand Rapids: Discovery House, 2000), 669.

Day 25: Who Are You Fighting for?

1. Laurence Gonzales, *Deep Survival: Who Lives, Who Dies, and Why* (New York: W. W. Norton, 2003), 180.

Satisfied

Discovering Contentment in a World of Consumption

Jeff Manion

Why does a contented, satisfied life feel so evasive? What deep hungers drive the reckless purchasing habits, out-of-control accumulation, and crazy consumer lifestyle for so many of us? And why are we often driven more by what our neighbors own than what will truly make us happy?

For many in the recent economic financial crisis, a series of lifestyle adjustments became necessary as hours were slashed at work and paychecks diminished. Vacations were simplified or canceled. Even important purchases had to be delayed, and any extras were put on hold.

In the midst of paring back and cutting down there lies the critical question: Will a spirit of resentment and complaint invade our heart, or can deep inner joy prevail, even as our dreams seem to fade? Is it possible to live a deeply satisfied life as possessions and opportunities slip away?

Followers of the Christ, living in the first-century world, also wrestled with issues related to material longings. For Christians living in Ephesus, Philippi, and Laodicea, the tendency to find their identity through accumulation and comparison was alive and well. These powerful longings are addressed in numerous places in the storyline of Scripture—a storyline that points us toward material and financial sanity and the pathway to true abundance and deep satisfaction.

Satisfied will draw richly from seven passages of Scripture, exploring the way in which these messages were received by the original readers and the way these passages can transform the way we view wealth, accumulation, and ultimate contentment today.

Available in stores and online!

Satisfied Study Guide with DVD

Discovering Contentment in a World of Consumption

Jeff Manion
with Christine M. Anderson

Why is a contented, satisfied life so evasive? What deep hungers drive the reckless purchasing habits, out-of-control accumulation, and crazy consumer lifestyle for so many of us? And why are we often driven more by what our neighbors own than what will truly make us happy?

In this DVD-based Bible study, popular communicator and pastor Jeff Manion provides an inspiring and transformative vision for living a deeply contented life in the midst of our consumer-driven, materialistic, and often shallow culture. In light of our surroundings, Manion asks a critical question: Is it possible to live a deeply satisfied life, one of great inner joy, even as dreams seem to fade?

Satisfied draws richly from seven passages of Scripture, exploring the way in which these messages were received by the original readers and how these passages can alter the way we view wealth, accumulation, and ultimate contentment today.

This study guide contains video notes, individual or group reflection questions, and between-session personal projects enhancing your journey through each of the video sessions on the enclosed DVD, taught by Jeff Manion.

Available in stores and online!

The Land Between

Finding God in Difficult Transitions

Jeff Manion

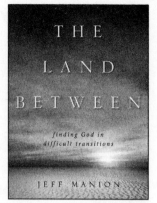

Author Jeff Manion uses the biblical story of the Israelites' journey through the Sinai desert as a metaphor for being in an undesired time of transition. After enduring generations of slavery in Egypt, the descendants of Jacob travel through the desert (the land between) toward their new home in Canaan. They crave the food of their former home in Egypt and despise their present environment. They are unable to go back and are incapable of moving forward. Their reactions provide insight and guidance on how to respond to God during our own seasons of difficult transition.

The Land Between provides fresh biblical insight for people traveling through undesired and difficult transitions such as foreclosure, unemployment, uncertainty, and failure. Such times provide our greatest opportunity for spiritual growth. God desires to meet us in our chaos and emotional upheaval, and he intends for us to encounter his goodness and provision, his hope and guidance.

A four-session DVD study with discussion questions is also available.

Available in stores and online!

The Land Between: A DVD Study

Finding God in Difficult Transitions

Jeff Manion

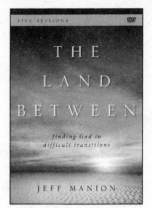

In *The Land Between*, pastor Jeff Manion uses the biblical story of the Israelites' journey through the Sinai desert as a metaphor for being in an undesired time of transition. After enduring generations of slavery in Egypt, the descendants of Jacob travel through the desert (the land between) toward their new home in Canaan. They are unable to go back and are incapable of moving forward. Their reactions provide insight and guidance on how to respond to God during our own seasons of difficult transition.

The Land Between is a five-session small group Bible study providing fresh biblical insight and hope, guidance, and encouragement for people traveling through undesired and difficult transitions —foreclosure, unemployment, uncertainty, and failure. Such times provide our greatest opportunity for spiritual growth. God desires to meet us in our chaos and emotional upheaval, and he intends for us to encounter his goodness and provision, his hope and guidance.

In *The Land Between*, you will learn:

- How to respond to God during your times of transition and difficulty
- How to find God in your pain and trust him in your waiting
- That the land between is essential for faith transformation and growth

Available in stores and online!